weed

420 things you didn't know about Cannabis

or remember

~ I.M. STON

Adams media

Avon, Massachusetts

Copyright © 2009 by F+W Media, Inc.
All rights reserved.
This book, or parts thereof, may not be reproduced in any form without permission from the
publisher; exceptions are made for brief excerpts used in published reviews.

Published by
Adams Media, a division of F+W Media, Inc.
57 Littlefield Street, Avon, MA 02322. U.S.A.
www.adamsmedia.com

ISBN 10: 1-4405-0349-4
ISBN 13: 978-1-4405-0349-8

Printed in the United States of America.

J I H G F E D C B A

Library of Congress Cataloging-in-Publication Data
is available from the publisher.

marijuana leaf © iStockphoto/Enjoylife2, joint © iStockphoto/itayuri, burn holes © iStockphoto/
khoj_badami, smoke © iStockphoto/Kasia75, paper © iStockphoto/billnoll

This book is available at quantity discounts for bulk purchases.
For information, please call 1-800-289-0963.

contents

CHAPTER THREE *Pot Etiquette* 27

CHAPTER FOUR *the company you keep* 37

CHAPTER FIVE *double-check what your sources tell you* 52

CHAPTER SIX *A PSA brought to you by THC* 62

CHAPTER SEVEN *ganja survival guide* 77

CHAPTER EIGHT *the highs of being high* 91

CHAPTER NINE *this is you on drugs . . . any questions?* 106

CHAPTER ELEVEN *the weed facts that will freak you out* 126

CHAPTER TWELVE *light up, camera, action* 137

CHAPTER THIRTEEN *mixed weedia* 148

CHAPTER FOURTEEN *celebrities and politicians who got higher in life* 167

CHAPTER SEVENTEEN *oh, the places you'll go . . . or avoid* 205

Introduction

In some ways, life as we know it hasn't changed since the 1930s—
there are still those out there who will tell you high tales worthy of
Reefer Madness (1936). But you know better than that, even when
you are high. This book reinforces the fact that you have done no
wrong by smoking a bong. We'll also prove that misconception that
potheads can't learn—they just need a subject that matters to them.

In *Weed*, we have compiled 420 different things that any cannabis
connoisseur should know and love about hashish. Basically, we've
been there, smoked that, and will advise you like an older sibling
who has made mistakes so you don't have to. Whether it's dealing
with buzz killers or coming down from a paranoid episode, we give
you the essential 411 (plus 9) that will directly contradict everything
you "learned" in DARE class. However, that DARE officer was a huge
loser and buzz killer, so perhaps you didn't want to be anything like
him, and started smoking pot to show him who really was in charge

of your life (just in case you can't tell, we really hated our DARE officer).

Oh, so your parents have informed you nothing good comes from smoking pot? Well, relax and toke up, because we got your back. From movies like *The Big Lebowski* (fun game: take a hit every time we mention this movie in the book) to the benefits of legalizing it like saving the economy, you're covered with this grasstastic guide.

Also, you know how one of your friends still makes that tired joke from *Half Baked* where he asks you if you ever did something "on weed"? While we recognize it was funny when Jon Stewart as the Enhancement Smoker said it in 1998, we promise that joke doesn't appear in this book. No need to thank us—just pass the bowl, man.

CHAPTER ONE

the cliff's notes
guide to weed

Word Origins You Thought You Would Never Know

"This is like if that Blue Oyster shit met that Afghan Kush I had—and they had a baby. And then, meanwhile that crazy Northern Light stuff I had and the Super Red Espresso Snowflake met and had a baby. And by some miracle, those two babies met and fucked—this would be the shit that they birthed."

—Saul, played by James Franco, in *Pineapple Express*

1. Schwag: The Other Green Weed

If the stuff in your bag looks flaky and green and like it should be sitting on top of a plate of spaghetti sprinkled with cheese—you're smoking schwag. Like the scrod of the cannabis kingdom, schwag is whatever cheap stuff your dealer can get his hands on that day, and pawn off on you to get fried. It tastes bad. Its high is not that great. And it should only be purchased if you're sixteen, you're broke, or you're dumping it on a plate of spaghetti.

2. Kush: Rapper's Delight

This strain of cannabis is so revered that it was romanticized in verse by one of the century's foremost lyricists—Lil Wayne in "Kush." This particular type of marijuana is a favorite of the rapper as well as many other weed aficionados. Known for its sweet smell, Kush also packs quite the punch with a high level of tetrahydrocannabinol (THC). First cultivated in the Hindu Kush Mountains (which is where it got its name), this variety of weed (classified as *Cannabis indica*) may be going through a bit of an identity crisis with a number of prevalent crossbreeds, hybrids, and variations. One thing's for certain though, you know you've made it in the marijuana game when Weezy's name-dropping you in his hook.

3. Purple Haze: Wander Weed

You may think that this is another song-celebrated strain, but—according to Jimi himself—the song "Purple Haze" is not about weed, or any drug for that matter. Instead, the title comes from a strange dream in which the rocker was lost wandering under the sea as a purple haze surrounded him. The weed, however, does have a purplish tint to its hairs and leaves, providing plenty of reason for it to take on the colorful moniker. And it may very well leave smokers feeling as if they too are wandering around under the sea in a purple haze, just like Hendrix.

4. G-13: Government-Issued Grass?

This is the conspiracy to end all conspiracies—if you're a stoner. It's believed that the U.S. government cultivated the G-13 strain for marijuana research purposes. How do you know this is true? Well, the *G* obviously stands for "government" and the *13* represents the thirteenth letter of the alphabet, *M*, which stands for "marijuana." Get it? Government Marijuana. While the only real backup to this legend is some support from *High Times* magazine, it doesn't take anything away from the breed's potency. A pure *Cannabis indica* strain, G-13 has a rather bland taste but causes quite the body high. Clearly a sign that the government bred it so that it could be used to keep stoners sedated enough to be force-fed antidrug propaganda.

5. Skunk: The Dank with the Stank

What do you think is the most noticeable quality of a marijuana strain called skunk? This type of weed has a very pungent smell, both in nugget form as well as when smoked. An indica and sativa cross, it's often used in the breeding of new marijuana varieties because of its potency. This is the kind of stuff that requires some time set aside to smoke, because it will leave you assed out on your couch, laughing hysterically at the drop of a hat, drooling over the fast-food commercials on television, but will also zap you of any motivation to get up and get food. Thank God for delivery.

6. Panama Red: Endorsed by Jerry Garcia

Jack Byrnes (Ben Stiller): If I set you up, do you think you can spike it, Focker?
Greg Focker (Robert De Niro): Well, I would have to get pretty high.
Jack Byrnes: I bet you would, Panama Red.
—*Meet the Parents*

Even De Niro knows how to spot a stoner when he sees one. His character's dad-to-son-in-law jab highlights the use of this strain's name as a common '70s synonym for pothead. The name Panama Red was bestowed on this breed because it hails from the sunny Central American country and has a reddish-brown hue. Beyond the red hue, the reference in *Meet the Parents*, and the Jerry Garcia song with it as a title, Panama Red is known for its strong psychedelic high, so make sure you're prepared for its crazy potency.

7. Bubbleberry: Weedalicious

An example of crossbreeding at its finest, Bubbleberry came about when the Bubblegum strain was bred with a kind of weed known as Blueberry, creating a type of cannabis that could have easily come straight out of Willy Wonka's candy factory. The intense flavor that's produced by this tasty race of marijuana has a bubblegum aftertaste with a distinct fruity tang. And beyond its flavorful bang, this hybrid strain packs a potent punch that will blow you away.

8. Northern Lights: Newbie Delight

This shit grows like, well, a weed. A hearty variety of marijuana, Northern Lights is very forgiving when grown indoors and therefore is a good selection for novice growers. And more important than the fact that it's resilient during maturation, it will get you fucked up. Pure Northern Lights is hard to find nowadays as it's often crossbred to create hybrid variations, but if you're able to get your sticky fingers on some, it will leave you seeing stars. A one-hit wonder, the strain gets its name not from the aurora-borealis-inducing high, but from the sparkling effect of the trichomes and crystals that cover its buds. Whatever the case may be for its naming, it doesn't take away from the fact that this is some dazzling dank.

9. Ice: Bling for Bongs

This cannabis variety keeps it cool with a thick coverage of crystals on its buds. A new-generation strain, its THC level is certain to keep smokers frozen in place (and time) on their couch. The plant's large buds have a strong aroma and are a rather dank and dazzling accessory to any pothead's favorite piece—if he has the money to shell out for such a top-shelf strain. Definitely worth its price, Ice's potency and ridiculous high will have you blazed enough to actually appreciate the artistic achievements of Vanilla Ice's *To the Extreme* . . . and to laugh at that joke.

10. White Widow: Watch Your Back

If and when you get your hands on this dank bud, be prepared to mourn the loss of hours—if not days—of your life. A Cannabis Cup winner, White Widow's a crossbreed between the *indica* and *sativa* species and provides an unbelievable high. Its name comes from the whitish tint caused by the plant's plentiful trichomes and its ability to incapacitate. Like preparing for battle with any master, you should train on some less-potent pot before trying to take on the Widow. This will help you appreciate its power when it takes you down. Because it will take you down.

The Roots of Weed

"So what is the name for it? I mean we all know
it's called the bionic, the bomb, the puff, the black,
the sensie, the cronic, the sweet Mary Jane, the shit, the
bomb, the ganja, the reefa, the bad, the buddha, the
home grown, the ill, the maui-maui, the method, the pot,
the shake, the skunk, the stress, the whacky, but is there
any other terms that parents should be aware of?"

—Ali G, played by Sacha Baron Cohen, on *Da Ali G Show*

11. Cannabis: Hands-Down Your Favorite Plant

This is the scientific name for the flowering plant that is pot. It's from the Greek
word *kánnabis*, originally a Scythian or Thracian word. There are three species
of the cannabis plant: *Cannabis sativa*, *Cannabis indica*, and *Cannabis ruderalis*.
The name cannabis refers to the entire plant, though only the flowers, buds, and
leaves of the plant can be smoked or eaten to produce a high. The rest of the plant
is referred to as hemp and, as you'll learn in Chapter 8, hemp is regularly used to
produce paper and clothing.

12. Marijuana: Officially Tied to Mexico

If you were to search for the exact etymology of the word *marijuana*, you would be left with an unknown origin. Its roots are in Mexican Spanish, and it is thought that the term came to popularity by American leaders to highlight that pot was a Mexican threat that had to be stopped. The word was originally used to refer to the cannabis that Mexican soldiers smoked as a medicine. *Marijuana* refers specifically to the flowers, buds, and leaves of the cannabis plant. Interestingly enough, unlike most other slang terms, *marijuana* is now an official word for the drug and is used in documentation and news articles on it.

13. Ganja: Thank Southeast Asia for This One

If you were thinking that because *ganja* rhymes with *ninja*, so the word *ganja* probably comes from the ancient art of kung fu, you are wrong. Now that that's out of the way, the term *ganja* actually comes from the Sanskrit word *ganjika*, and in modern Indic languages, it's *ganja*. It is generally used nowadays to refer to marijuana that is especially potent because the type that is native to this region, *Cannabis indica*, was found to be a much stronger kind of weed when introduced in America. Like most slang terms for weed, ganja was used as a way to talk about it without everyone around you necessarily knowing what you were talking about. Today this wouldn't work, as ganja has become so ingrained in the American language that it is immediately recognized as an alternative term for marijuana.

14. 420: It's about That Time . . .

Have you ever wondered why you actually smoke at 4:20 every day? There are many urban legends floating around about where exactly it originated. Some say it's the number of chemicals in marijuana, which isn't true; the number of chemicals changes depending on the plant, so it could be anywhere from 300 to over 400 chemicals. Some say it's the police code for smoking pot, but that's not true either—there is no 420 police code at all. The generally accepted story is that 420 began as a way for pot smokers at California's San Rafael High School in 1971 to discretely communicate each other that it was pot-smoking time. The students coined the term to alert their friends that it was, to put it simply, time to get high, and it grew into a common term related to smoking pot.

15. Hemp: Eco-Friendly . . . and Illegal

Hemp, from the Old English *hænep*, is the term for the roots, stalks, and stems for the cannabis plant. It is the earliest-known woven fabric, and for generations it has been regularly used to make paper, clothing, lighting oil, medicine, and construction materials. Unfortunately, in the United States, antimarijuana laws do not recognize a difference between marijuana and hemp, and it is therefore illegal to grow unless the grower is granted a license for it from the DEA, which is, as you can imagine, very difficult to get. Hemp grows faster, produces stronger and longer-lasting paper than trees, needs no pesticides or herbicides, and does not pollute rivers with chlorine like wood pulp mills do.

16. Mary Jane: Fewer Syllables Than Marijuana

Nope, Tom Petty didn't come up with this term with his song "Mary Jane's Last Dance" (although, now it's stuck in your head, isn't it?). Mary Jane is a takeoff on the word *marijuana*. Some theories say that if the word marijuana did come from two Spanish names, it would be the Spanish equivalents of the names "Mary" and "John," not "Mary" and "Jane," but there is no conclusive answer to this. Mary Jane has spurred the slang term *Aunt Mary*, which is also used in reference to weed.

17. Herb: Cooks Up Extra Nice

Here's one you might know: "herb" became a slang word for pot because of the simple fact that cannabis is an herb and dried weed looks like an herb. Marijuana falls well within the Merriam-Webster definition of herb: "a seed-producing annual, biennial, or perennial that does not develop persistent woody tissue but dies down at the end of a growing season." This is also where the terms *weed*, *tree*, and *grass* come from: they all refer to the basic fact that marijuana is reminiscent of these plants. Some things in life are just that simple.

18. Reefer: Madness, Indeed!

Reefer is another name for a marijuana cigarette. The name is thought to have derived from the Spanish word for marijuana, *grifa*. Also, you don't have to be high to know that sounds funny because the word *marijuana* was Spanish in the first place, but it's true. It is now one of the most common terms for the drug. The term was popularized with the 1936 release of the infamous movie *Reefer Madness*, which was a cautionary tale of a boy who becomes addicted to marijuana and the ensuing lives that are shattered as a result.

19. Skunk: Potent Smell, Higher Than High

Skunk refers to a type of weed created in the 1970s, which is still one of the most popular strains of the drug today. Around that time, Spanish weed (*Cannabis sativa*) was becoming more scarce due to American efforts to destroy the marijuana crops in Mexico (thereby cutting off the supply to Americans). Because of this, travelers began bringing in marijuana that was native to Afghanistan and India (*Cannabis indica*). Soon a hybrid of the *sativa* and *indica* species of cannabis was created that had a much higher potency and a stronger smell than the previously existing kinds. Because of this olfactory potency, this new creation was named "Skunk #1" (or "skunk" for short), thus, you and your friends can smell its stinky presence.

20. Hashish: Arabian Etymology

Hashish (sometimes just called "hash") comes directly from the Arabic word *hashish*, meaning "grass." Hashish is extracted from the trichomes (glandular hairs) of the cannabis plant and is generally in a dark-colored paste form with various degrees of thickness. If you ingest it, hashish will provide you with the same potency as other parts of the cannabis plant. Hashish can be used in all the same ways that marijuana is used, such as in pipes, bongs, joints, and cooking.

CHAPTER TWO

*hAVE yOUR wEEd,
ANd EAT it too*

Smoke It, Eat It, Drink It

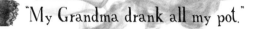 "My Grandma drank all my pot."

—Alex, played by Allen Covert, in *Grandma's Boy*

21. Roll It with Your Homies

The most popular way to smoke weed, the joint is the hamburger of marijuana consumption. You can dress it up with flavored rolling papers, go high-quality by filling it with a potent strain, or just sink into one (and your couch) by laying down some grass and spinning it up tight with your index fingers and thumbs. Whether you go with the always-hip Zig-Zag papers, or the tasty Juicy Jay's, or the trendy vegan sheets made by RAW, a joint is a joint is a joint (unless it's mixed with some tobacco—in which case it's a spliff). Pay respect and roll one up right now.

22. B Is for Bowls

Every connoisseur has his specialty glassware. Beer lovers have their pilsners. Scotch lovers have their tumblers. Pot lovers have their bowls. A bowl is the must-have accessory for any stoner, and is a perfect way for you to express your personality. Visit your local head shop and peruse its various offerings. Bowls come in a variety of sizes, colors, and degrees of ornamentation. However, don't jump at the first one you see, as other smokers will judge you based on your bowl.

Pick the one that works best for you, and remember what the last Knight of the First Crusade told Indy: "Choose wisely."

23. It's Also for Bongs

The next step up from the bowl in terms of pothead accessories is the bong. Like bowls, bongs come in a variety of sizes, materials, colors, and degrees of fuck-up-ability (the better your bong, the better your high). For the marijuana novices out there, a bong is a vertical pipe with a closed base that holds water and has a two-part slide (which is made up of a hollow female stem piece and a smaller-in-diameter male piece that has the bowl on one end and is inserted into the female piece by the other). Pack the bowl, light it up, inhale from the top of the pipe, and then pull the male piece out while inhaling to clear the chamber: congratulations, you just took your first bong hit.

24. . . . And for Blunts (Potheads Love Their Bs)

Nothing says Sunday like sitting on your stoop with a blunt and a 40. To roll your own and celebrate the Sabbath, go out and purchase a cheap cigar like a Philly or Dutch Master. Lick the cigar to get it moist and then slice it down the middle. Work the tobacco contents out of the wrap carefully so you do not tear it. Then fill it with your pot of choice. Roll the wrap tightly, lick up the seam, and run your lighter's flame up and down the length to seal. Throw on Dre's *Chronic* and get comfortable. Light. Smoke. Repeat.

25. Ooey-Gooey Sticky-Icky

Mmm pot brownies . . . as major a staple in stoner culture as apple pie in Americana. When you feel like turning your sticky-icky into ooey-gooey, look no further than the mixing bowl in your kitchen (that's the thing you and your friends thought would make an awesome slide attachment for that imagined twenty-five-foot bong). Recipes vary and you're welcome to put a personal touch on your own batch (maybe stir in some peanut butter chips). Follow the instructions on the side of the packaged brownie mix, except when they call for butter, use a refrigerated and hardened version of the bud butter you'll find in the Lobster Marijuana entry.

26. Buon Appetito, Mon

The Caribbean meets the Mediterranean in this delicious dish. You can match your culinary skills with your cannabis love with rasta pasta—the perfect entrée to serve during 4/20 celebrations (see Chapter 16). While your pasta cooks in a pot of boiling water, heat a jar of your favorite sauce in a pan, mixing in half a cup of chopped marijuana (or if you're the love-child of Woody Harrelson and Martha Stewart, add marijuana to the ingredient list of your homemade pasta sauce, if it isn't there already). After simmering the sauce for about twenty minutes in order to release the weed's THC, pour it over the pasta to create a mouth-watering, mind-altering meal.

27. Lobster with Bud Butter

Who says cannabis can't be classy? Break out the plastic bibs and get ready to dine in stoner style. While the lobster itself won't be steamed in weed (though getting it baked before you drop it in its Jacuzzi isn't a bad idea), the dipping butter you use to indulge in the tasty shellfish will be infused with marijuana. Melt up a batch of bud butter by dropping two sticks of butter into a small pot over medium-to-high heat; stir in half an ounce of shake or finely ground weed; continue stirring until the melted butter has a green hue; pour through a very fine strainer or piece of cheesecloth to separate out the leaves. Crack open your red friend, dip the meat in the cannabis concoction, and enjoy.

28. Scooby *Doobie* Doo

We all know what went on in the Mystery Van when that group of meddling kids wasn't busy tracking down creepy groundskeepers. And that those Scooby Snacks were just the quartet's way of including their canine pal without him slobbering all over their joints. But now the snacks aren't just for the four-legged. You can cook up your own batch by following your favorite oatmeal cookie recipe (without raisins), and substitute the called-for amount of butter or margarine with the refrigerated and hardened butter from the "Lobster Marijuana" entry. You'll be ready to solve all sorts of mysteries after you eat a few Snacks—except for the one about where the day went.

29. Tea-H-C

This ain't your grandma's tea . . . unless she enjoys partying like Alex's grandmother in *Grandma's Boy*. If you want a brew that will really mellow you out, try boiling up a special teapot of pot tea (get it?). Since THC is not very water-soluble, you'll want to add one cup of whole milk with two cups of water and three tablespoons of ground marijuana. Let the milk/water/weed mixture boil a little longer than you would a normal pot for tea and then pour it through a strainer into your favorite mug. You can even add an actual teabag for flavor. Enjoy with crustless cucumber sandwiches and scones as you discuss who would win in a fight between Queen Elizabeth and Mothra.

30. Piece of the Middle East

Ah, the gifts of the Middle East—falafel, crude oil, and döner kebabs, just to name a few. The one to focus on here, however, is the hookah (though döner kebabs are a serious munchies satisfier). It's a version of a water pipe that has you (or you and your friends if it's a multihose pipe) inhale through a hose which causes the tobacco and marijuana to roast by drawing heat from a burning charcoal at the very top of the pipe. You might hear some clamor that it's an ineffective way to smoke since some of the weed burns without actually being inhaled. Those people obviously don't realize how cool it is to pretend you're the caterpillar from *Alice in Wonderland*. Suckers.

Satisfying the Munchies

Kenny Davis (Harland Williams): Hey, if I'm not back in 10 minutes call the police.

Thurgood Jenkins (Dave Chappelle): If he's not back in 10 minutes, we're calling Domino's!

—*Half Baked*

have your weed, and eat it too 39

31. Twinkle Toes

No one is quite sure what's in a Twinkie, but no one really cares either! All we care about is the fact that nothing hits the spot like a Twinkie when you've been hitting it up. There's just something about the forever-spongy exterior and the vanilla filling that explodes in your mouth. Twinkies are so popular that, according to Hostess.com, Bill Clinton, who smoked but never inhaled (yeah, right), even put one in a time capsule that was sealed during his presidency. He probably just wanted to see if a stoner would eat it when it resurfaces in fifty years.

32. Break and Bake, Courtesy of Toll House

Remember making cookies with your mom when you were a kid and begging to lick the bowl? Good times! Even better is eating raw chocolate chip cookie dough after a day of a different kind of baking. Don't feel like you have to make up a batch before you smoke. Just go to the store, buy a premade roll, cut the wrapper halfway down, and enjoy the cold, chocolaty concoction. Most store-bought cookie brands don't contain raw eggs, a carrier of the bacteria salmonella, so eating it is even safer than eating what you'd make from scratch. What are you waiting for? Head over to your local supermarket and pick up a little piece of heaven in a tube!

33. Pizza, Pizza!

There's no getting around the face that everyone loves pizza. It's an American staple. According to *Parade* magazine a whopping 94 percent of the U.S. population loves pizza, and 93 percent of Americans eat at least one pizza per month. How much of that pizza is consumed by those who have just partook in pot has not yet been determined. Cold pizza, lukewarm pizza, pizza straight from the oven that's so hot you burn your mouth on it—you really just can't go wrong. Plus, how many other foods can you order that someone will actually drop off at your house?

34. Yo Quiero Nachos?

Cheesy, spicy, messy, and all around good. We must be talking about nachos! Let's be clear here: the tortilla chip is really only a crunchy carrier for all the cheesy, chili goodness that's piled on top of them. You need some way to get them to your mouth without a fork after all. You can really put anything on top of a nacho. There are recipes for chocolate nachos, cheesy nachos, breakfast nachos, and many more. If you dream it, or if you have tortilla chips and a bunch of crap in your fridge, it can become reality. And, really, what's better than eating everything in your house while you're high?

35. Fry It Up!

There are many ways to get French fries onto your plate. You can eat them frozen, heat them up in your microwave or toaster oven, throw them on a sandwich, or pile them high on top of a plate and use them to make nachos (after all, cheese, sour cream, and chili go well with fries too). But the best way to get fries if you're fried is to get them from McDonald's, Burger King, In-N-Out Burger, or some other fast-food chain. They're hot, they're relatively fresh, they're salty, you can dip them in anything you want (like a milkshake), and you can get them with a whole bag of junk food.

36. Betcha Can't Eat Just One

What can you say about potato chips? They almost speak for themselves. You really can't eat just one—and why would you want to? You might not be sure why anyone would want to put a salty hard chip in a cottonmouth, but that's the last thing on your mind when on the search for munchies! Maybe it's the grease that settles into your stomach, the rise in your blood pressure after you finish off the chips with your BFF, or the satisfying crinkle of the package as you reach your hand in again and again, but if you bought a dime bag, you're going to want to stop for a bag of chips, too. May as well be prepared!

37. Pickles: Craved by Stoners and Pregnant Women Everywhere

When is a cucumber not a cucumber? Obviously, when it's a pickle! Maybe nobody has ever been jonesing for a cucumber after smoking up, but seep that cucumber in a vat of salty vinegar for a month and all of a sudden it's a different story. Maybe it's that salty goodness that you crave. Maybe it's the satisfying crunch. Any type of pickle will do: sweet pickles, sour pickles, bread and butter pickles—take your pick. However, nothing beats the juicy crunch of the huge, juicy pickles you get out of the barrel at the deli counter.

38. Got Milkshake?

There's a reason milkshakes are a favorite midnight beverage. Honestly, what's better than a milkshake when you've finished your last joint for the night, or even if you're just taking a break between bong hits? You can get one in any flavor (chocolate, peppermint, banana, etc.); they're cold to help you cool off your smoky throat;

thick, which means you can savor them instead of ripping open that bag of Doritos; and mainly, they're just all-around delicious. Even better, they're great to dip things in, which is almost a requirement for a munchie. Maybe you can open up that bag of Doritos after all.

39. The Classic: Doritos

We've already said that Doritos are a great dipping food, and they are! Dip them in a milkshake? Sure! But nothing beats crispy, cheesy, neon-orange Doritos dipped in a sweet, cold, creamy Ranch dressing. This sweet and savory combination gets a thumbs-up in any stoner's book. Cool Ranch Doritos try to take out the middleman by including the ranch dressing on the chip, but Cool Ranch Doritos are just trying to shortchange you. You may be high as a kite, but you can still dip your own chip, thank you very much!

40. Dangerously Cheesy Cheetos

You may think that paranoia would set in when a stoner hears something is dangerously cheesy, but apparently that logic doesn't hold water when that "dangerous something" ends up to be dangerously cheesy Cheetos. It doesn't matter which type of Cheetos you personally prefer. The puffs or the twisted snacks are equally as satisfying. According to FritoLay.com, Cheetos now also come in a variety of flavors—Chili Cheese, Flamin' Hot Limon, Natural White Cheddar, Crunch Cheddar Jalapeño—the list goes on and on. It doesn't matter which bag you pick up at the local 7-11—each flavor is equally satisfying when you have the munchies.

Bongology

Alison Scott (Katherine Heigl): I'm sorry
I told you to fuck your bong.
Ben Stone (Seth Rogen): It's okay, I didn't.

—Knocked Up

41. DIY Bongs and Bowls

Most containers, many kinds of fruits and vegetables, office supplies, etc., can
be used to create bongs and bowls. For a bowl, you need to make three things in
your container of choice: a "bowl" to put the weed into, a mouthpiece to suck the
smoke out of, and a hole called a "carb" to clear the smoke out of the chamber
between hits. For a bong, you need a container that can hold water, a hole below
the water's surface to attach a tube or straw to, at the other end of which will sit a
bowl or joint, a carb above the surface of the water, and either the main opening of
the bottle or another hole for the mouthpiece.

42. An Apple a Day . . . Keeps the Jones Away

When you use an apple (or any other hard fruit of choice), you not only gain a
sweet taste to the smoke but also have a biodegradable and easy-to-dispose of

bowl. Take a pen and push it through the apple at a downward angle starting toward the top of the apple and a bit off center—one side will be your mouth-piece, the other side the carb. Remove the pen and insert it again on the top of the apple, making sure to meet the first hole in the middle of the apple. Carve out the top of the hole you just made into a cone: this will be your bowl. Pack your weed and light it up, sucking the air out of the first hole you created.

43. The Water Bottle Bowl: Stay Hydrated–and High

Another simple yet effective way for you to smoke up. Take a water bottle and carve a hole in it for the bowl. Cover it with tinfoil and poke holes in it. Carve another, smaller hole in the side of the bottle for your carb. Use the normal drinking opening of the bottle as your mouthpiece and, voila, you have yourself a water bottle bowl. And you're recycling, too!

44. The Water Bottle Bong: Recycling at Its Best

This is the easiest way to make a bong. Take a two-liter bottle and punch a hole about three inches from the bottom. Attach a tube or straw to this hole and insert a joint or a bowl in the other end of the tube. Make sure the hole is airtight. Closer to the top of the bottle, punch another hole that can easily be covered with your finger; this will serve as the carb. The top of the bottle will be your mouthpiece. Fill the bottle with water until the lower hole is at least an inch under water. When you suck in through the mouthpiece (with the carb covered), it will draw up the smoke from the tube.

45. A Can Will Work in a Pinch

Are you in a rush to smoke and don't have time for complicated techniques? Then the can bowl is the perfect thing for you. Take an empty soda or beer can and indent it a bit on one side. Poke a handful of tiny holes on the flat part. The already-existing mouth of the can will serve as your mouthpiece. Put your weed over the holes you poked, light it up, and enjoy. If you want a carb on the can to clear the smoke out between hits, poke out a hole on the side.

46. The Party Bong, Courtesy of Poland Springs

Here's a design that's great for situations where multiple people want to smoke. Take a twenty-liter plastic water cooler jug and drill four holes toward the top. Insert tubes into these holes to create your four mouthpieces. Drill a hole in the cap just big enough for you to put a bowl into. Attach a tube to the bottom of the bowl that's long enough to reach the bottom half of the jug. Make sure all the holes are airtight. Fill the jug half-full of water and commence smoking. What you have here is a ten-liter chamber of smoke for four people to enjoy at once.

47. Mountain Dew Gravity Bong

The gravity bong is out of the world, killer sweet. Take a Mountain Dew two-liter soda bottle (or another soda bottle). Cut the bottom off and drill or cut a hole through the cap large enough to put a bowl into. Take a bucket or other large container and fill it with water. Tightly insert the packed bowl into the hole of the cap. Submerge the two-liter bottle about three-quarters of the way into the water, light the bowl, and slowly pull the two-liter up out of the water until the bottom is almost to the water surface. Quickly remove the cap and, placing your mouth to the opening, inhale the smoke as you lower the bottle back into the water. The pressure created by this action pushes the smoke into your lungs in a smoother manner than inhaling from a joint or bowl by itself.

48. A Highlighter High

When you make a pipe out of a highlighter, you are not only making an easy pipe, but also creating an inconspicuous way to carry a pipe. First, hollow out the highlighter and cut off the ends so that you can see through it. Then, drill or carve a hole into the highlighter toward the end that is large enough to hold your weed; cover that hole with tinfoil and poke tiny holes in it. Lastly, sack in your weed and smoke away. You can use one of the ends as your mouthpiece and the other as your carb. When using highlighters, pens, or other materials made of plastic, you might literally burn yourself out of being high if the plastic begins to melt.

49. Coconuts for Cannabis

This is a bit more complicated than other bongs you could fashion, so be prepared to do more work on this one, preferably while you're still sober. First, take a coconut and split it into two pieces, drain the milk, and remove the fruit (for a more authentic Jamaican coconut "chalice," remove the milk and fruit from one hole without splitting open the coconut). Let the shell dry and glue it back together. Carve three holes in the shell—one each for the stem, bowl, and carb. Insert your stem and bowl of choice into the holes, making sure they fit in snugly. Variations of this involve sanding the inside and outside of the shell for a cleaner smoother look or using the device as a water bong.

50. The Bong Goes Back to Its Roots

The word *bong* comes from the Thai word *baung*, meaning a cylindrical wooden tube, pipe, or container cut from bamboo, so why not go old school and make a bamboo bong? Take a length of hollow bamboo about two feet long. Cork one side with a piece of wood or some other plug and sand the other to make a smooth mouthpiece. Because bamboo can be porous, coat the inside of the bamboo shaft with wax. Drill a hole for the stem and insert a tube, or if you prefer it to be aesthetic, a hollow wooden dowel. Use epoxy or glue that isn't toxic to adhere the dowel. Attach a bowl to the end of the dowel. Now you've got yourself a useful, historical work of art!

CHAPTER THREE

POT ETIQUETTE

The Dos and Don'ts of Dealing with Dealers

"I love my FedEx guy cause he's a drug dealer and he don't even know it . . . and he's always on time."

—Mitch Hedberg, standup comedian

51. Don't Expect Lots of Idle Chit-Chat

Drug dealers are the ultimate neighborhood businessmen, glad to perform an entrepreneurial chore in the community. They'll be happy to make small talk with you . . . for at least the first ten seconds of the deal. Remember, though, that you're there on business, not a social call, and they've probably got other customers waiting. Respect their time. Express a polite interest, but be prepared for the fact that they may be a bit hazy on specifics when you ask if their vacation plans include a trip to Jamaica in the near future.

52. Don't Mention Your Relative Who Works for the DEA

Don't mention that your cousin who works with the DEA happens to be visiting you this week and "would he be surprised if he could see me now!" Matter of fact, your cousin probably has suspected you for some time and regularly raided your stash since he arrived on Monday night. Don't think about your cousin. It's probably best to refrain from mentioning to the dealer that he works for the government. Or that you even have a cousin. Leave the cousin at home where he belongs. The dealer isn't interested in him.

53. Don't Try to Pay with Postdated Checks

Also, you should refrain from trying to negotiate the price in yen, euros, lira, or Canadian dollars. You just need to take enough cash to pay for the weed. You may think it's funny to show up with a giant bag filled with all the pennies you've been saving for weeks, but the dealer won't see the humor. You must resist the temptation to ask if he takes MasterCard. He doesn't. Nor does he accept Visa, Diner's Club, or your Sears charge card. And this is one time when you can safely leave home without your Amex.

54. Don't Ask Your Dealer to Hang Out

While your dealer *might* be interested in accompanying you to a performance of *Swan Lake* or the Police Benevolent Association annual dinner dance, remember that they have other concerns at the moment. So should you. There's a time for culture and a time for other things. And if you run into your favorite dealer at an Ingmar Bergman film festival, don't ask him about the last time you met. The situation is fraught with possible embarrassment for the both of you. It's best to glaze over it and just return to your seat.

55. Do Mind Your Manners (But Keep It Brief!)

There's no need for outright rudeness (in fact, there's every call for excessive politeness during a deal). This is the world of retail, after all. Most dealers appreciate courtesy. You would, wouldn't you? However, both of you know that in this world, time is money. Dealers will appreciate you more if you're a repeat customer, unarmed, alone, and pay quickly in cash. Rules to live by.

56. Don't Make Any Sudden Movements

A calm demeanor and low, steady voice are more likely to end the transaction happily for everyone concerned. So, don't look over their shoulder and shout loudly, "Hi, Officer Ferguson!" or "Yo! Seriously big drug deal going down here!" If you've got an old police siren in your car that you've been longing to set off—don't. Many dealers are sensitive and become nervous when confronted with such behavior. They also disapprove of sudden bright lights, particularly when shined in their faces, and voices amplified by bullhorns.

57. Do Keep Phone Hookups Short and Sweet

When your dealer answers your telephone call, avoid saying cheerfully, "Hi! Is this Marcus's House of Ganja and Good Times Where the Weed Is Strong and the Women Are Hot?" Keep your phone call short and simple. In the world of drug dealing, less is more, and discretion is held in high regard.

58. Do Dress for the Occasion

Something simple in dark knits with plain, clean blue jeans is indicated. Above all, you don't want to wear any of the following to your drug deal: a bright orange prison jump suit; a T-shirt that says in four-inch-lettering "Drug dealers do it in the dark"; a waterproof jacket that has "Police" written across the back; a pair of coveralls, a straw hat, and a large button that says "Kiss me, I'm from Kansas!"; Hare Krishna orange robes and sandals; or anything made of lime-green polyester (since drug dealers have aesthetic sensibilities like anyone else and there's no reason to shock them unnecessarily).

59. Don't Try to Negotiate the Price

What are you thinking? This isn't your local Chevy dealership. The dealer isn't going to ask you to wait a minute while he steps into the back room and talks to his boss to see what they can do to get you to walk out of here with this fine, first-class weed. Get some perspective, for God's sake! This is a freakin' drug deal. The price is set, already! It's simply supply and demand—capitalism at its finest. Just pay it, say thank you, and get moving.

60. Do Follow Your Dealer's Lead Without Question

Take a moment to locate the exit nearest you. Some exits may be behind you. In the event of an emergency, there is absolutely nothing around you that can be used as a flotation device. You're completely on your own. Should the deal suddenly experience a drop in pressure, make your way calmly and quietly to the closest exit. Then run like hell.

Mind Your Manners

"Mr. White? Are you smoking weed? Oh my God! Wait a minute, is that my weed? What the hell, man? Make yourself at home, why don't you?"

—Jesse Pinkman, played by Aaron Paul, on *Breaking Bad*

61. Always Pay for What You're Going to Smoke

If you didn't bring your own weed, you have an obligation to offer money for the weed that is there and not be a mooch (see Chapter 4). Everybody might *say* it's cool that you don't have the money, but in reality, they really don't want you around and don't respect you. Hit up an ATM, steal from your family, whatever you have to do to make sure you have money. If for some reason your friends say you don't have to pay for your share of weed, you better make it up to them the next time you see them by bringing some sweet cannabis.

62. Never Slobber Over the End of a Joint

When you are sharing a joint or bong, never, ever leave it as if it has been molested with a one-sided French kiss. This is disgusting, selfish, and completely unethical. You would be basically claiming the joint or bong for yourself and challenging your friends to taste your spit if they want to get high. When anything is passed around again, you will be constantly skipped. Also, if you're interested in making out with someone in the room, your chances are drastically reduced because that person will not want to make out with a sloppy-kissing, selfish jerk.

63. Never Pack a Bowl Without Asking

If you've shared in the expense of weed with someone else, you are obligated to make sure they're ready to smoke before you pack a bowl. Although you're always ready to smoke, your friend might not be properly prepared (some dudes have crazier rituals than Nomar Garciaparra's batting routine). Nevertheless, you need to be patient and ask before lighting that bowl. However, your friend should show equal politeness, so if he doesn't get prepared in a timely manner, you have every right to just keep asking him if you can light it as many times as kids ask "Are we there yet" in a car.

64. Never Talk about Anything Too Serious

Smoking weed isn't a time to talk about life-changing decisions and serious events that are happening in the world. First off, you should be using cannabis as an escape from reality; second off, you're ruining everybody else's buzz; and third off, see a psychiatrist. However, if something happens that will prevent you from imminent and future smoking, aka cops or parents, you should definitely discuss the best course of action. More than likely though, your friends still won't want to become serious, so be careful.

65. Never Bogart

Named after actor Humphrey Bogart because he often would leave a cigarette in his mouth but not smoke it, to "bogart" is to keep a joint to oneself and not pass it along. Consider yourself in a community that shares joints in order to bond with each other. If you hold on to the joint, you're disappointing your fellow man and might as well stay at home and smoke by yourself. Humphrey Bogart's Rick Blaine had to let Ingrid Bergman's Ilsa Lund go in *Casablanca*, and she was smoking hot, so in comparison, passing along a joint isn't so bad.

66. Never Volcano

When you volcano, you exhale into a bowl, thus exploding bong water and weed ash all over the floor, and, in the process, pissing off everybody in the room. Now, if someone is smoking for the first time, you can accept a certain grace period where, okay, they volcanoed but they didn't know any better. However, if an experienced bong hitter volcanoes, that person is just being a jerk and you have every right to throw him out of your place. Also, when you're drunk and want to get high, you should consider that, like drinking and driving don't mix, drinking and bowl smoking don't mix either.

67. Never Yell at Someone Who Is High

Yelling at someone who is high is like kicking kittens—it's cruel and unusual punishment for harmless creatures. Whether the yeller is trying to mess with someone to make up for his own delusions of being Sam Kinison or he is actually seriously yelling at the person, it is just wrong to scream at someone who is too high to fight back. This could lead to the person's increased paranoia (see Chapter 9) and a bad trip. To put it into context: do you remember the drill sergeant yelling at Private Pyle (Vincent D'Onofrio) in *Full Metal Jacket*? Well, it's like that but also *being high*.

68. Never Bring Skunk Weed to a Party

You're invited to a pot party and you should bring some kind of weed, but you figure there will be so much weed, who will notice your skunk weed? Well, the answer is everybody and they will all recognize that you're a cheap SOB just by the smell of the skunk weed. Seriously, if you don't have the money to buy respectable weed and have no choice but to buy skunk weed, that's fine, just leave it at home. If Dante's *Inferno* had been based on cannabis, the person who brought skunk weed to a party would be in the last circle of hell.

69. Never Raid Someone Else's Cabinets When You Have the Munchies

When you're at a friend's house, you should adhere to certain rules that would apply if you weren't high. You wouldn't normally open every cabinet in the kitchen looking for Doritos even though your friend keeps telling you he doesn't have them, so don't do it when you're high. If you have a seriously consistent munchies problem, then supply your friends' cabinets with your own food; also, since he's letting you use his cabinets, you should do what you learned in kindergarten and share your snacks.

70. Always Be the Funny Person

When you're high, you should be lighthearted and ready to tell a joke at any point. If you're not original, just quote lines from the weed movies in Chapter 12. If you're still not funny, you can still manage to be a fun person. When someone breaks out into a song, you could either start singing backup vocals or making trumpet-like noises. You can also prevent not being funny by avoiding lame jokes. For example, don't ever pretend a bong is a penis. Yes, everybody knows a bong is phallic, so move on with your life.

CHAPTER FOUR

The Company You Keep

Sniffing Out a Narc

> Iris (Jodie Foster): Are you a narc?
>
> Travis Bickle (Robert De Niro): Do I look like a narc?
>
> Iris: Yeah.
>
> Travis: I am a narc.
>
> —*Taxi Driver*

71. Two-Faced Tommy, the Informant

Somehow, at every party, he is there. The informant hangs out with potheads, listens to the same music they do (he totally digs the Flaming Lips, but only on an artistic level), and enjoys the same things in life as stoners. Like Doritos. But only half of the time, because he differs in one small way. He does not smoke, and neither do his other friends. He seesaws between parties and he is enough of a two-faced narc to give those wretched *others* the low down on everyone in the room without hesitation. And if you share a class or an office with the informant, one day you will walk in and find disapproving stares from those around you. He finally did it: he told *everyone* what you were doing this weekend.

72. No-Name Shmoe, the Guy Nobody Knows

Here's another character, just like the informant, you must always be on the look-out for. In fact, you can bet money that he came to the party with the informant . . . or maybe it's just paranoia. The guy nobody knows is always there. Nobody can vouch for him, nobody can figure him out, nobody knows who brought him, and nobody can tell if he can be trusted. He can't. Is he a friend of a friend? A boy-friend? Good God, a parent? A cop?! That's his whole thing. A man of mystery. One thing is for sure, though: you should never break out the stash until he's gone. Just in case.

73. Nick the Narc, the Overly Enthusiastic to Get High Guy

The night is off to a good start, everyone is in a nice, chill state, and someone mentions pot. Just casually mentions it. Suddenly, the overly enthusiastic guy jumps on that idea like a fiend. Now it's all he will talk about. No matter what new topic comes up, he jumps right back to smoking. "We should totally just roll a fat one and smoke up." "Let's just get stoned." "Who's got some weed?" "Who wants to throw down? I know a guy that will hook us up." This should be a fire alarm going off in your head with self-preservation on your mind. Only a narc could be *that* excited about getting high. No pothead gets that excited—it takes too much energy.

74. Sally, the (Vindictive) Ex

It's not a concept foreign to weed. A vengeful ex will do just about anything to get back at her former partner. She could key your car. Or throw a rock through your window. Or, she could take a more vicious approach. You know how you and your buddies hang out on Wednesday nights and smoke up? Yeah? Well, so does your ex. And your ex is *not* above calling the cops and pretending to be a neighbor who looked over and saw some dope fiends next door plotting a night of depraved drug use.

75. Mr. Johnson, the Old Guy Who Lives Next Door

Technically, he doesn't need to live next door, or anywhere near you, really. But he probably does. There is no breed of human on the planet—not cops, not judges, not DEA officers—more infuriated by the fainted whiff of marijuana than an elderly man. In fairness, it could be an elderly woman as well, but elderly males are generally far more grizzled. His logic is: "It's disgusting what this country has become. Dope fiends roaming around in nice neighborhoods. Someone needs to do something about it!" Watch out.

76. Pax, the Stereotype

He wears tie-dyed T-shirts and hemp necklaces, he wears sunglasses indoors, he never shuts up about how "mad chill" Burning Man was last year, and his car has pot leaf stickers all over it. *Half Baked* is his favorite movie ever, *man.* He talks about it all the time, and he always seems high, but you have never actually seen him smoke. Something is up with him; he is just a little too typical. Well, that's because he's an undercover cop. In reality, he's never even smelled weed before, let alone smoked it. His entire preparation for his role consisted of watching *Super Troopers* twenty times and learning to say "man" at the end of every sentence.

77. Robbie Jr., the Little Brother

Any stoner with a younger sibling knows just how vindictive they can be. Say your friends all come over one day and your little brother wants to hang. He makes a pest of himself, asks too many questions, and eventually overstays his welcome. After you throw him out, you break out that new pipe and a bag of mids. Later that night you find yourself having a family meeting against your will on the grounds that "Billy told us he saw you and your friends smoking marijuana this afternoon." This happens every day. It is always safer to assume that, yes, your little brother or sister is going to narc on you.

78. George, the (Square) Roommate

Whether it's in college or a prude taking residence in your multibedroom apartment, you might eventually take residence with someone who does not approve of your lifestyle. Naturally, this can only lead to disagreements, fights, and ultimately revenge. You will be up at 3 A.M., blaring that new trip-hop album, burning Hot Pockets, and smoking out of the tub that you decided to turn into a gravity bong. In other words, Thursday night. Eventually, the roommate will decide he has had enough. Then the cops are at the door, and guess who is standing there with them, arms crossed, shaking his head at you?

79. Nick the Narc, the Twenty-Questions Guy

The twenty-questions guy is another one who makes an appearance at just about every party. He isn't there to smoke, but he sure is excited about *you* smoking, isn't he? Again, you have no idea who he is, maybe a friend of a friend of a friend. As soon as the bong is seen on the table, he's just fascinated. "What's this part do?" "Dude, smoke, I want to see how it works." And so on. You know him. All signs point to "narc." Why else would someone who doesn't smoke be so adamant about you showing your hiding spot, breaking out your stash, and doing something illegal?

80. Wyatt, the Dude Who Just Doesn't "Get It"

"I don't get it. Why do you like to just sit around and do nothing on a Friday night?" "I must be missing something, *The Big Lebowski* just isn't that funny." "Why do you spend so much money for such a small amount?" "You guys really want to go to Wendy's *again*?" Never trust this guy. Anyone with that kind of rationale is out to ruin your night, and he will eventually narc you out to his uncle, who's a cop, just so you get a slap on the wrist and learn some sort of life lesson. Leave him at home and go to the laser show.

Buzz Killers

Dr. Gregory House (Hugh Laurie): I don't remember you being this bitchy.

Dr. James Wilson (Robert Sean Leonard): The Vicodin dulled it. In the sober light of day, I'm a buzz kill.

—House

81. Mikey, the Mooch

You know that guy—he invites himself over to your place the second he hears that you have some pot. He just wants "a few hits" but never offers any money and never returns the favor. You're not his dealer and this isn't a situation for charity, dammit! You have a few options: pass the mooch on to someone else with "better stuff;" pretend you're not home; or give him oregano so that he thinks your weed sucks. However, do *not* give him your hookup's contact information—he'll end up owing your weed source and that has only negative consequences for you.

82. Frankie, the Faker

As you pass around a joint, you observe one person doesn't actually inhale. Nobody else notices this at first, but soon everybody knows this person is a faker. The faker is quickly recognized as trying too hard to be a stereotypical pot smoker, constantly overcompensating for his lack of highness, and using being high as an excuse to be a jerk. Once identified, this attention whore must be stopped. You should say something that no stoner would actually say and see if the faker goes along with it, and keep escalating these comments until the faker becomes self-aware and shuts up.

83. Eddie, the Emotional One

The emotional one thinks smoking weed means expressing deep emotions about relationships and work. This is not only a downer but also completely defeats the purpose of getting high. The emotional one needs to know the smoking boundaries. Just because people are getting together to smoke weed doesn't mean this emotional one can bear his soul like he's at an AA meeting. Blast your stoner music or the sound of the TV while it plays a stoner movie to blatantly point out you aren't listening to emo music or a chick flick. If this doesn't work, you need to be as insensitive as possible until he cries himself to sleep.

84. Sam, the Straight-Edge Kid

You were just being polite by inviting the straight-edge kid ("straight edge" meaning no drugs or alcohol) so he wouldn't feel left out, but now he is just sulking in the corner and snickers every time someone coughs. Ian MacKaye, who coined the phrase "Straight Edge" with his old band Minor Threat, once said, "In 1983, we put out a record called *Out of Step* and in one of the songs I articulate that 'Straight Edge' is not a strict set of rules for people to follow and that I'm not interested in that idea at all." So, the straight-edge kid should remove the stick that is up his ass and let others enjoy themselves.

85. Stevie, the Snob

Like a person who just wants a cold beer like Sam Adams after a tough week, you don't really mind the equivalent in quality when it comes to weed. However, there is the self-described weed connoisseur who will criticize any cannabis that isn't from the wild forests of Africa and harvested by the native children. He has had better cannabis and lets *everybody* know it. So, tell him to bring his own weed if he doesn't like yours. Of course, this will lead to him saying that he wants you to pitch in for his golden weed. Tell him no, you'll stick to your cannabis that gives you a satisfying high. He would probably rip you off with skunk weed anyway.

86. Ollie, the Oppressed Smoker

When he is high, the oppressed smoker talks about how unjust and difficult life is for him. Granted, yes, there are injustices in the world, but smoking weed is neither the time nor the place to address them. As Dave Chappelle said in one of his standup acts, "Every time I smoke weed with my black friends, all you talk about is your trials and tribulations. I'm sick of that shit. I got my own problems, that's a waste of weed. I'm smoking weed to run away from my problems, not take away from yours."

87. Erin, the Ex

The ex is an awful buzz killer for so many reasons. If you have the same friends, you have no choice but to occasionally see the ex when you want to smoke up. Also, while you're just trying to get high, the ex might try to pick a fight with you about something you're too high to remember or care about. Also, the ex might bring in a new partner, making your smoking experience both more paranoid and awkward. All you can really do is get more high so you can rationalize the ex's existential state of being in the world, man.

88. Fran, the Former Addict

The former addict probably has done every drug imaginable (you don't quite know for sure). If fact, you're not really sure what he's doing there at all. If, in some mystical way, there is any truth to that whole "marijuana is a gateway drug," this dude is probably screwed once he takes his first hit. He's obviously jonesing because even when he reminisces about all of the foolish acts that he did while speedballing, he doesn't actually display any shame. You probably should hide the rest of the weed and get this addict and whomever brought him out of there ASAP.

89. Sunbeam, the Smelly Hippy

Being a hippy is fine with all of that peace and love. A hippy should be a weed smoker's ally in the anti-war on drugs. However, someone else smelling like rotten milk is just a huge distraction from the smoking task at hand. Yeah, a hippy did have a reputation to uphold—back in the 1960s. So you can tell him that nobody is judging him if he takes a shower once in a while. Also, you can help the smelly hippy rationalize this decision by telling him he can use that natural soap shit. Basically, everybody smoking should be inhaling the cannabis instead of the hippy's nasty combination of sweat and cat urine.

90. Paul, the Parent

You know family should be a huge part of your life, and you should be grateful for them. However, parents just shouldn't smoke weed with you and your friends. Yeah, they might think they're bonding with you, but for you, it is like time traveling back to elementary school when you didn't want them to walk you to the bus stop because the other kids would laugh at you. Your parents were hip and jive (and whatever other retro terms) when they smoked back in the 1960s. That's fine and all, but they are supposed to be the authority figures who you're rebelling against. Also, the realization that they were actually cool at some point in their lives will not only ruin your buzz but also cause major therapy down the line.

Stupid Cannabis Crimes

"A 14-year-old Indiana girl was arrested after she came to a middle school with a handgun, ammunition, and six small bags of marijuana. Man, Dakota Fanning's growing up so fast!"

—Amy Poehler, on *Saturday Night Live*

91. Do You Have Change for an Ounce?

As hungry for a Big Mac and large fries as you'll ever be, never try paying for the feast with weed. Shawn Pannullo learned this seemingly simple lesson the hard way when he tried to barter food for weed in a Florida McDonald's. Just after midnight, Pannullo ordered through the drive-through, but left when the cashier refused to take the trade. She called the police and gave them the description of Pannullo's car. This led to his arrest a short time later and a charge of possession of marijuana. And to top it all off he went to jail hungry.

92. Cop Foiled by Pot

It happens to the best of us. You pull someone over and steal their weed, bake it into brownies that you eat with your wife, you freak out and think you're dead, and call 911. Or maybe not *all* of us, but it did happen to former Dearborn, Michigan police officer Edward Sanchez. Sanchez and his wife ate the stolen-pot-filled brownies and proceeded to have such a bad trip that they thought the pot might have been laced with something. "I think we're dying. I think we're dead. I really do," Sanchez told the dispatcher during his five-minute-long call. "Time is going by really, really, really, really slow." Sanchez resigned from his post and was not prosecuted.

93. It Really Isn't Easy to Be Green

You know better excuses than the following guy, so never end up like him. An Iowa man claimed that the large amount of pot that police officers found in his car was not for smoking, but for compost. Police reported that the man had several large bags of Mary Jane in his car, and when asked about it, he said his only intent was to turn the stuff into compost. The officers didn't buy his load of . . . compost, and arrested the man. He was charged with processing marijuana with intent to distribute.

94. You Can't Make It Much Easier on the Police

A Washington State man was smart in looking to hide his stash before he appeared in court. Unfortunately, his hiding spot was not ideal—under a bush outside the sheriff detectives' window. The detectives saw Eugenio Anthony Colon hide the container in the bush and confronted the man, who was in the courthouse for an unrelated matter, while he awaited his court appearance. Colon told the detectives that he didn't realize they were there or could see him. With defenses like that who needs lawyers?

95. You Should Be Worried Your Kids Are Messed Up When . . .

Three surprisingly dedicated teens in Houston were looking for something to smoke out of when they decided digging up a grave and stealing a skull to turn it into a bong would be a good idea. According to the teens, they spent two days digging up the grave with gardening tools to remove the skull from the rest of the skeleton of an eleven-year-old boy who died in 1921. One of the boys told the police about the grave robbery when being investigated for a car robbery. The boys were charged with abuse of a corpse and vehicle break-in.

96. Candidates for the Dumbest Criminal Award

What do Michael Omelchunk, Stephen Knight, and Cory Oxtoby Have in Common? They all called the police to report that their weed had been stolen. Omelchunk's stash was stolen from him in his apartment by two armed men. The police found more weed that wasn't stolen and arrested him. Knight also had thieves break in, but he was hogtied with Christmas lights before they stole his stuff. Police also found more drugs in his place and arrested him. Oxtoby was robbed at gunpoint while he was trying to make a sale in a Wal-Mart parking lot. He was also arrested when he called police to report the theft. Make sure you never challenge these clowns for the Dumbest Criminal Award.

97. Selling Weed on Craigslist—Bad Idea

Sometimes in life you should make the extra effort instead of taking the easy way out. Steven Zahorsky couldn't be bothered to actively try to sell his weed and instead made a posting on Craigslist for the product. His post worked—he received a response from a man looking to buy three-quarters of an ounce of weed. Unfortunately, that man was a Stamford police officer. The officer responded, saying he was part of a painting crew that was looking to buy some weed and arranged to meet Zahorsky at a highway rest stop, where they made the exchange and he arrested Zahorsky.

98. Weed Googles

Don't think that merely because you have your pot crop hidden in a cornfield you're good to go. Police in Zurich, Switzerland, got a lucky break when Googling the address of two farmers they were investigating as part of a larger drug operation. When the Google Earth satellite map came up, the officers clearly spotted the two-acre large patch of weed that was being grown inside of a cornfield. The find helped in the investigation of the larger drug operation that led to sixteen arrests and the seizure of 1.2 tons of marijuana.

99. Yeah, the Economy Is Bad and All, But Still . . .

If you're caught growing weed, you should try to get on the authority's good side, unlike the following dude. A man in Gasquet, California, is suing the Del Norte County Sheriff's Office for lost profit over the destruction of the ninety-three mari-juana plants that were taken from his house when he was arrested under charges of marijuana sales. Kirk David Stewart claimed the plants should have been returned to him when the case was dismissed because he was found to be in com-pliance with the Compassionate Use Act of 1996. Because the sheriff's department destroyed the plants, Stewart claimed he should get the fair market value for the plants, which would have totalled several hundred thousand dollars.

100. The Perfect Place to Grow Weed

If you're going to grow pot, you shouldn't plant it in the plantation of a nunnery—religious karma is a bitch to deal with. In Athens, Greece, two men approached two elderly nuns there and offered to help with their garden. Instead of planting tulips and roses, however, they planted thirty cannabis plants. Police received a tip about the garden and found the plants. The nuns who thought the weed was merely "large decorative plants" were not arrested.

CHAPTER FIVE

double-check what your sources tell you

Where to Grow Weed

"I think people need to be educated to the fact that marijuana is not a drug. Marijuana is an herb and a flower. God put it here. If He put it here and He wants it to grow, what gives the government the right to say that God is wrong?"

—Willie Nelson, musician

101. Amsterdam, Man

Cannabis coffee shops? A weed museum? It's no surprise that Amsterdam draws 4.2 million tourists—mostly serious stoners—each year. But for those who are lucky enough to call the capital of the Netherlands "home," not only is it a great place to toke, but also there's no better place to grow the grass. Because using pot is so widely tolerated, you can pretty much get away with cultivating your crop where and when you choose. Just don't get too greedy and grow a field's worth of weed. The law "strictly" states: Soft drugs as cannabis in all its forms (marijuana, hashish, hash oil) are legal under the condition of so-called "personal use."

102. Cali's Emerald Triangle

American-made weed is as important to the lifeblood of the United States as GM, Chrysler, and Ford. But smoking hashish won't need or get any kind of government bailout anytime soon. And when it comes to the great United States, you can't find a better place to grow the stuff than sunny California. Growers say that prime conditions include lots of sunshine (preferably that will hit all sides of the plant), warm (but not too warm) temperatures, and a built-in consumer base looking for product all around. So, hit up those surfers for some stash.

103. Vermont Isn't Just for Skiing and Fishing

Contrary to popular belief, cannabis can be grown as far north as Canada. And if you've ever been to Vermont, you know this bordering state has its fair share of weed-loving laxers. In fact, for a city that is only a forty-five-minute drive from clearing customs, Burlington is perfectly placed to take in a Canadian crop. Home of the University of Vermont, deemed *Princeton Review*'s number 3 "Reefer Madness" school in America, this modern-day hippie hangout town can also be considered the munchies mecca—the Ben & Jerry's Factory is only a fifteen-minute bike ride away.

104. Across the Border, Mexico (If You're Crazy)

It is widely believed that weed grows wild in Mexico, but it's more likely that drug production in the country is carefully ruled by the hundreds of drug lords and traffickers who find remote regions, genetically improve plants, and protect their crop by all means. So if you need to get stoned so bad that you're willing to risk the swine flu for a little high-flying fun, do your research and avoid remote moun-tainous regions, like Michoacán. In Michoacán, cartels have been battling over lucrative marijuana plantations for years, and President Felipe Calderón has been conducting raids to restore order and stop the violence.

105. Your Backyard Bonanza

You've already learned that Cali is the best place to grow weed in America, so if you live there—congrats on your lucky and hopefully lucrative local product. But no need to go paranoid if you live somewhere outside the sunshine state: people sow seeds in every great state. When it comes to your own backyard though, there are a couple of things to keep in mind. Weather aside, watch out for thiev-ing neighbors, peeing dogs, and "helpful" spouses who want to garden with you on the weekend. One way to make a few pot plants work in your existing garden, without getting caught, is to plant them under or within a bush of another kind. Think hydrangea or lilac.

106. Build a Water Park in Your Basement

According to many sources, if you want a quality plant—and you don't need a great amount of grass to go around—indoors, hydroponics is the way to go. While making and maintaining a successful hydroponics system might be hard (and way too hard to explain in this book) the key ingredient to making your basement flowers flourish is the seeds. Experts suggest going with something called the sinsemilla, or the unfer-tilized "female" plant. These groovy gal growths don't produce seeds that allow the plant to use more energy on the thriving THC . . . long story short—stronger weed.

107. A Greenhouse Is for Grass

Most experts suggest using soil instead of hydroponics if you're an inexperienced grower. In fact, growing weed in soil will probably make you feel more like a legit gardener than if you set up an elaborate water-shooting-pipe-system anyway. So, if you're an aspiring green thumb and you're serious about your stash (who wouldn't be?), what do you do? The best way to grow grass in soil is in a greenhouse. If the conditions are right and sun streams through the glass while the Martha Stewart in you is consistent and controls the water flow, you'll have thriving plants before you know it.

108. In a Broken-Down Car on Your Lawn

Don't live in the city with a shared greenhouse available? Or do your neighbors keep stealing your stuff? No problem. Improvise. You know that ratty run-down hunk-a-junk in your yard? If you clean it up just right and make a couple of changes, you can turn that rusty piece of metal into a first-class, personal greenhouse. The trick is to replace any broken windows and "install" a proper sunroof. If you have to saw the roof off completely to get the effect, that's fine—just lay a piece of glass on the existing frame and what d' you know? You've got yourself a greenhouse.

109. Take a Hike for a High

Too nervous to have any stash right in your own backyard? It's a bit of a risk, but you can take your seeds to the local state park or neighboring wooded area and plant them among the pines. Try to find somewhere secluded and easy-but-not-too-easy to get to. The trick here is to remember where you left your goodies. You might take that Boy Scout training to heart and leave yourself a trail. Just make sure your signals aren't going to wash away in the rain or get eaten by the wooded creatures, and you're good to go. That is, until some lucky hiker happens upon your hash.

110. Fire Up on a Fire Escape

If there aren't any woods for miles, what's a weed whiz to do? Chances are if you're a city slicker, you've got yourself a fire escape. How often do you use the emergency exit from your flaming building anyway? Make use of that precious space and add some square footage to your place. Even though the outdoor ledge is technically in plain sight of pedestrians and neighbors across the way, no one will bother your grass garden and your stash is surely to thrive in the sunny streets of the big city.

The Best Places to Buy Weed (and the Places You Should Never Score)

Logan Echolls (Jason Dohring): Didn't your dad say that the cigar store's a front for drug dealers? I mean, that's gotta be something.

Veronica Mars (Kristen Bell): Or not. Sometimes a cigar store is just a cigar store.

—*Veronica Mars*

double-check what your sources tell you   **57**

111. Any Relative of a Police Officer Is Just a Narc-in-Training

Have you ever helped your mom or dad out at work? Thought so. Keep that in mind the next time you think of buying weed off of the son or daughter of your local police chief. You may be thinking to yourself, "But if we get caught, her dad is much more likely to help us out." Right? Wrong, wrong, wrong. Most likely, she's just helping her dad clean up the potheads in town—yeah, that's you. So do yourself a favor and stay clear.

112. A Playground Is Tempting with Those Swing Sets

This is a really bad idea. There's a special place in prison for people who do drugs around kids—and cops will be sure you land there if they nab you with a baggie. So while it may seem like the playground offers lots of hiding places—with the tube slides and jungle gyms—this is pretty much the *last* place you ever want to buy weed or get high. Besides, isn't there something a little creepy about getting high at such an innocent place?

113. Concerts: These Are the Real Deal (Oh, Supposedly They Have Music Too)

Concerts are the holy grounds of getting high. The Mecca would be your outdoor summer festival. It's probably the only occasion where most people *are* high. Even if you don't have a ticket to the concert, go hang out in the parking lot. Look for the most spaced-out looking people you can find—and stay away from them. You don't want to know what they're on. Find the next-most-spaced out people, and see if they have a quarter to sell. It's the best reason to go to a concert.

114. Medical Supply Companies: Come on, You Saw That Scene in *Half Baked*

While weed is still illegal, there are some people with certain medical conditions who have their doctors' permission to smoke. So you're perfectly healthy? That shouldn't stop you from sampling the highest-quality, medical-grade pot. Stop by a designated weed supplier and see if you can find someone who has more pot than he needs—then offer to pay him for a bud. If they don't need it all, then an illness (or your lack thereof) shouldn't be reason to stop you from catching a strong buzz.

115. Carnies—No, Bad, No, Don't Think about It!

Repeat after me: *never buy weed from a Carnie*. These people are paid to rip people off. *See if you can shoot the moving clown! Step right up and see if you can drop the clothespin into the world's smallest milk bottle.* You do *not* want to be involved in any sort of monetary transaction—especially not on their home turf. While it may be tempting to ignore my advice since all carnies look like they just blew a joint, tread carefully here. After all, you can't exactly tell the police you got ripped off buying a bag.

116. The Biggest Douche in Your Neighborhood

When looking for a weed hookup, you should be even pickier than you are with the other kind of hookups. After all, the only way a one-night stand can go wrong is if she turns out to be a psycho and chains herself to your bed. With weed, there's a lot of room for disaster. So even if the asshole down the street has the cheapest weed you've come across since high school, you should steer clear. You're bound to end up with a bag of oregano.

117. Your Friendly Local Hippie Might Smell, But That Can Be Overlooked

Ding ding ding! We have a winner here. As far as pot sources, there's no better person to buy pot off than a hippie. They're all about peace, love, and getting high. So while they may be a little on the unwashed and stinky side, they're also friendly and often the holders of some pretty trippy weed. Be sure to keep your mellow around these guys—quick movements and loud noises will kill their buzz.

118. Jail Has at Least One Benefit

Okay, you may not *choose* to buy weed in the big house. But if you happen to find yourself behind bars, it's one of the easiest places to get high. With all of the inmates (many of them in there for drug-related offenses), you're sure to find at least one guy on your block who has some weed to trade. Just be sure not to get caught, because if TV prison shows are at all accurate, you do not want to end up in solitary confinement.

119. Local College Campus: The Kids Aren't All Right But That's All Right

Colleges are the perfect storm of weed: young kids who like to party and get high. Not currently in college? No problem. Wander on to campus on a sunny day and look for the hippies tossing around a Frisbee. Or wait until a weekend night and go to one of the dozens of houses with people spilling on to the front lawn. Added bonus: college kids are most often broke, so you may be able to talk them down.

120. Friends of Your Parents Are as Good as Giving Your Weed Away

So you've heard rumors that your buddy's dad pays for their ski house with a little side Class D distribution. As tempting as it may be (hey, you know he won't rip you off), don't go there. He may tell your parents, or worse, tell your buddy that you're a bad influence and forbid him from hanging out with you. So while there may be a convenience factor that's hard to deny, the payoff doesn't outweigh the risk.

CHAPTER SIX

A PSA brought to you by THC

Gateway Drug, My Ass!

"It really puzzles me to see marijuana connected with narcotics . . . dope and all that crap. It's a thousand times better than whiskey—it's an assistant—a friend."

—Louis Armstrong, musician

121. Why Weed Is Better than Alcohol

The hangover. Just about everyone has been there. Sure, you may wake up with bloodshot eyes, cotton mouth, and an insatiable hunger for pancakes, but you probably never woke up half-naked behind the local watering hole in a puddle of your own fluids, and praying, just *praying* that crusty stuff on your face is your own vomit, because you stayed out for one too many hits. But one too many tequila shots is another story entirely. For this, weed will always be better than alcohol.

122. Why Weed Is Better than Crack Cocaine

Anyone who has ever spent time in any major city in America has run into him. The toothless, incoherent, wild-eyed, stuttering freak in the street. He's always spinning a yarn about how a few years ago, he was working a high-paying job, drove an Audi, and had a beautiful wife. Then, he blew his first line of that sweet powder off some unnamable region of a high-end stripper . . . and you know the rest. He'll be the first to tell you, "Shoulda stuck to the pot, man!" If he had, he'd be at home in bed playing Nintendo Wii on his 62-inch flat-screen TV.

123. Why Weed Is Better than Acid

Weed is better than acid for a whole lot of reasons, not the least of which is that you've probably never heard of anyone jumping out of a tenth-story window after lighting themselves on fire because someone "harshed their mellow." That kind of shit would just take way too much time and energy when you are stoned. Most stoners won't usually want to venture much farther than the cabinet with the Pop-Tarts after a few hits, let alone fight off invisible space demons and melting walls.

124. Why Weed Is Better than Crystal Meth

The myriad of reasons why being in the company of a pothead is more preferable than being in the company of a methhead explain in and of themselves why weed is better than crystal meth. First off, potheads can stop talking for more than three seconds without chattering their teeth to the point they're chipped and their gums are bleeding. Most importantly, however, is the simple fact that it just seems far more logical and desirable to be in the company of someone calmly tending to a few plants than locked in a room with an amateur "chemist" burning chemicals that if inhaled at the wrong time, may kill you, or worse yet, blow everyone in the room to pieces.

125. Why Weed Is Better than Heroin

How many of your favorite artists and musicians ever passed out and choked to death on their own saliva from smoking weed? Think about it. John Belushi, Janis Joplin, Chris Farley, Lenny Bruce, Mitch Hedburg, and the list goes on and on. Good luck finding a Wikipedia biography for a celebrity who died from smoking weed. William S. Burroughs, who was an opiate addict, wrote in the original introduction to his novel *Naked Lunch*, "I had not taken a bath in a year nor changed my clothes or removed them except to stick a needle every hour in the fibrous grey wooden flesh of terminal addiction." Nobody outside a 1930s exploitation flick can say that about weed.

126. Why Weed Is Better than Ecstasy

While smoking a blunt may give you a minor case of dry mouth, ecstasy likes to step it up, causing, according to a study at Rutgers University, "dehydration, hyperthermia, and heart and kidney failure." That alone makes weed better than ecstasy. You may insist on listening to Snoop Dogg of Rush records incessantly while high on cannabis, but, well, there's nothing wrong with that. Have you *heard* the crap that ecstasy freaks impose on the world? Deep Trance? House Dub? Seriously, you are already one step ahead of the game.

127. Why Weed Is Better than PCP

People still use this shit? We've all heard the stories of people freaking out and fighting groups of shotgun-toting cops with their bare hands on this stuff, or breaking through a brick wall with their head. According to a recent news story on Fox

News a man on PCP was arrested for "biting [his son's] eyeball out of his face and eating it." Weed is better than PCP because if you smoke enough, you can forget stories like that.

128. Why Weed Is Better than Huffing Paint Fumes

Remember middle school? If so, you probably knew at least one kid who did this on a daily basis. He either didn't know how to get weed or couldn't afford it, so he did the next "best" thing and huffed paint. Or glue. Or markers. Well, not only does that kill brain cells faster than hitting yourself in the head with a sledgehammer, but also it's not as fun. That is the reason middle schoolers do it. They just don't know any better. By the way, you know what that kid from middle school does now? No? He doesn't either.

129. Why Weed Is Better than Tobacco

Arguably, the only major difference between weed and tobacco is that cigarettes are legal and weed is not (for now). As comedian Bill Hicks once said, to paraphrase, the only difference is that tobacco is taxed, while weed costs Uncle Sam money instead of making him richer. The major reason why you should smoke weed rather than tobacco, though, is the small fact that, according to the American Cancer Society, each year "443,000 people in the United States die from illnesses related to cigarette smoking." Compare this to a study published in the *Washington Post* stating weed has "no association at all [to cancer], and even a suggestion of some protective effect." Let the facts do the talking.

130. Why Weed Is Better than That New Drug Your Cousin the Amateur Chemist Made

Without a doubt, if there's not one in your family, then there is at least one in a friend's family. The guy who got some sort of two-week online degree in something like chemical engineering and is convinced that with a few over-the-counter products, a Bunsen burner, and a lot of caffeine pills, that he is now qualified to produce synthetic drugs and sell them to the public. Soon enough he will want you to try it. For free, too. Who knows what is in it, but one can guaran-damn-tee that, yes, weed is better than that new drug your cousin with the online chemistry degree made.

This Is Your Brain on Drugs

"I now have absolute proof that smoking even one marijuana cigarette is equal in brain damage to being on Bikini Island during an H-bomb blast."

—Ronald Reagan, former President of the United States of America

131. Buying Drugs Equals Funding Terrorism

In the wake of the September 2001 terrorist attacks, you might remember that the Office of National Drug Control Policy debuted a series of ads that insulted the nation's collective intelligence by insinuating that buying drugs was equivalent to committing heinous acts of terrorism. "I killed mothers. I killed fathers. I killed grandmas. I killed grandpas. I killed sons. I killed daughters," a teenage boy says matter-of-factly in one ad. "Drug money supports terror. If you buy drugs you might too," the ad ominously proclaims as the boy goes on with his litany. There really isn't an excuse for these preposterous attack ads.

132. They'll Understand

The 2004 "They'll Understand" ad campaign was the Office of National Drug Control Policy (ONDCP) at its most melodramatic and sarcastic. In one ad, an unsupervised toddler wanders into her backyard, drops a toy in the pool, and presumably drowns while trying to get it back. The narrator chimes in, "Just tell her parents you weren't watching her because you were getting stoned. They'll understand." Another ad features a boy waiting forlornly by a curb. Turns out his brother was too busy getting high to come get him. But that's okay; the kid will understand, right? You, like America's youth, had a hard time viewing the ads because your eyes had rolled so far back in your heads.

133. Smoking Pot Will Make You Run Over Kids on Bikes

The first part of this ad shows a group of teenagers exiting a drive-through. A kid on a bike darts in front of the car, and they slam on the brakes just in time. In the second part of the ad, the teens have consumed so much marijuana that the entire car is filled with thick smoke. When the little girl pedals in front of their car, she gets flattened. The most common reaction to this spot? Uproarious laughter. You know you love slapstick. Needless to say, the ad was ineffective. A Texas State study reported that respondents questioned the girl's parents for letting her ride around a busy intersection unsupervised. Also, the ad was later spoofed in a 2004 episode of *The Chappelle Show*.

134. The ONDCP's 1999–2004 Advertising Failures

In 1998, the National Youth Anti-Drug Media Campaign was created and charged with the task of educating parents and teens about the hazards of drug use. Between 1999 and 2004, the government spent about $1 billion on antidrug advertisements. But then the government's own study of the ONDCP's ad campaign concluded that the ads actually made certain groups of kids more likely to try marijuana. So naturally, the Bush administration sat on the study for a year and a half before the public finally got wind of it. In the meantime, the ads continued to air, at a cost of hundreds of millions of taxpayer dollars. Yeah that's right—tax money that you could have spent on cheeba and Chef Boyardee.

135. Marijuana Affects Your Relationship with Your Dog

In 2006, the ONDCP unveiled a series of crude cartoon TV ads. The first few feature a glorified stick figure and his talking canine sidekick. The recurring theme is the dog's disappointment with his owner for being a pothead. Apparently, the ONDCP felt there was nothing quite like being shamed by your pet. In one of the spots, the guy even tries to get the dog to smoke with him, much to the dog's disgust. In another one of the spots, the guy's girlfriend subs for the dog. He lights up and she groans, "Not again." At that moment, a marijuana-free alien putters up in a spaceship and sweeps the girl off her feet. Yeah, and you're supposedly the one with "issues."

136. Nancy, Such a Naysayer

If you were a kid growing up in the '80s and early '90s, you couldn't avoid the slogan made famous by then First Lady Nancy Reagan, "Just Say No!" As the main weapon in the "War on Drugs," this taught young people that drugs are bad. But why does it always have to be so negative? A campaign based around "Just Say Yes!" would be so much more positive. Yes to the kid who wants you to burn it after school; yes to the hottie who passes you the pipe; and yes to the coworker who asks if you want to toke up during a break in a depressingly long meeting.

137. A Brain Omelet Actually Sounds Delicious

When you're high, your gray matter in *no* way resembles a sunny-side-up egg. Your brain on drugs is more like a perfectly cooked goat-cheese and asparagus omelet, with home fries on the side (mmm . . . home fries). Your brain on drugs is like egg salad seasoned with paprika and pickles (mmm . . . pickles). Your brain on drugs is like a bacon-egg-and-cheese sandwich on a toasted everything bagel (mmm . . . bacon). A sunny-side-up egg is just runny and gross. They obviously got it wrong, so why not get working on that egg sandwich?

138. Stoned Sonny, '70s-Style PSA

This PSA is so totally awesome, it's tough to do it justice by describing it. You should *really* Google it and see for yourself. However, if you're too lazy for that, here goes nothing: cue the acoustic guitar music, fade in, '70s brunette smoking a joint . . . '70s blonde spacing out . . . crazy candlepin bowler guy . . . dude with slick leather jacket driving a big old jalopy down a hill and getting out while the car is still moving then *car crash!* Fade to black, then: Sonny Bono, sporting a big frizzy 'do and shiny orange shirt, looking straight into the camera, very slooowly reciting how marijuana will destroy your teenage years and all meaning in your life.

139. "I Learned It from You!"

Another totally awesome late '80s ad that deserves mention here is the "I learned it by watching you!" ad. The kicker line: "Parents who use drugs have children who use drugs." If anything, weed would bring parents and children together to bond. Do you remember that scene in *Half Baked* where the dad is smoking weed from his pipe and wondering how he can bond with his kid, who is smoking cannabis in the next room at that very moment? You should definitely trust anything Dave Chappelle says about weed over pretty much anything else.

140. Burrito-Taster Ad

Truly perplexed as to *why* this ad from Above the Influence would deter you and your friends from becoming potheads; hell, it makes you want to become a god-damn *professional* pothead. Seriously, this job sounds a-mazing. Burritos are really delicious. The ad states: "Start earning now! Why waste the best days of your life going to college when you can become a burrito taster. Money, power and jet packs are some of the benefits that a certified Burrito Taster enjoys. That, and all the Burritos You Can Handle! Restaurants, motels, clubs, theme parks, and space stations are just a few of the places that need experienced Burrito Tasters. EAT THE GOOD LIFE!!!"

High Hazards

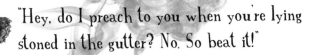

"Hey, do I preach to you when you're lying stoned in the gutter? No. So beat it!"

—Bender, voiced by John Di Maggio, on *Futurama*

141. Marijuana Sizzles Brain Cells

Tommy Chong (to say nothing of Ozzy Osbourne) would seem to be a walking advertisement for this hazard. But if you're looking for something a bit more informative, consider this: the main chemical in marijuana is something called THC (it stands for delta-9-tetrahydrocannabinol, if you're really interested). THC causes the reactions in body chemistry and functioning at a cellular level that lead to the experience of being high. One area of the brain that it affects is the hippocampus, the part that's involved in learning, memory, and mixing sensory experiences with emotions and motivations. Researchers have found that THC suppresses the information-processing system of the hippocampus. So, if smoking marijuana makes you feel stupider . . . well, that's pretty much what it's doing.

142. Grass Gunks Up Your Lungs

The basic point about weed here is that you're *smoking* it. In other words, it has a lot of the same effects on your lungs that smoking anything else does: it can cause bronchitis, emphysema, and ultimately, lung cancer. In fact, according to ThinkQuest.org, marijuana contains between 50 percent and 70 percent more cancer-causing chemicals than cigarettes. A University of California study (*www .canadafreepress.com*) reports that Mary Jane smokers inhale five times the carbon monoxide as do regular smokers. Marijuana smoking also boosts your chance of a heart attack by four times.

143. It Makes You Look Like Hell

Possibly you think that smoking grass will make you look like Johnny Depp in *Blow* or something. If so, you might want to think again. Among other things, excessive use of grass can lead to dry mouth, bloodshot eyes, and swollen eyelids. It can also elevate the risk of head and neck cancers. And we all know how attractive it is to go to a party sporting a big tumor on your neck! Not to mention the fact that since marijuana can lead to short-term memory loss, you'll probably forget to change your clothes, brush your teeth, or bathe. Now *that's* a pretty picture!

144. You'll Make Stupid Choices

A study of behavior among college students—who can use all the unimpaired judgment that's coming to them—found that heavy weed users suffered impaired judgment, learning, and memory skills. Research seems to show that those who smoke a lot of joints tend to score more poorly than those who don't. However, it's also true that the studies of this have focused on heavy users rather than casual users. Still, if you're going to be paranoid, this is as good a reason as any.

145. Weed + Munchies = Weight Gain

Let's be clear here: marijuana will not, in itself, make you fat. Overeating will do that. But smoking weed will stimulate your appetite. One of the effects of THC is to make food taste delicious. Any food—even Brussels sprouts. That's why when you smoke it, you get the munchies. And afterward, you sit and watch old episodes of *Gilligan's Island* on television and wonder how you never noticed before how totally hot Ginger was for the Skipper. So you're overeating junk food without exercising. Sounds like a good recipe for weight gain.

146. Say Hello to Hallucinations

Smoking pot can cause your brain to become more suggestible and prone to fantasies, such as the notion that *all* Adam Sandler movies are funny. If the grass you're smoking is particularly potent, the visions you have can become increasingly disturbing and paranoid. In all fairness, a lot of experienced users say that hallucinations are common only if you're smoking marijuana that's been laced with another drug. On the other hand, some people argue that hallucinations can be a good thing. So it's all a matter of perspective.

147. Weed Weakens the Immune System

Although some people argue that grass should be legalized as a way of treating the symptoms of AIDS and other diseases, a lot of medical folks suggest that when smoked in excess, weed can be harmful to people with compromised immune systems. Regularly using pot weakens your body's natural defense systems, including macrophages (cells that attack and kill invading viruses) and T-cells. If that's the case—and there's a lot of research to suggest that it is—smoking grass as a way of feeling better after chemotherapy is probably at least as damaging to your body as the chemicals themselves.

148. Smoking + Pregnancy = No Go

Most women know they shouldn't smoke cigarettes or drink alcohol while pregnant. But there's a myth out there that somehow this doesn't apply to grass. In fact, it does. Smoking pot during pregnancy can affect your baby in various ways, all of them not good. Studies have shown that children born when their mothers smoked weed have trouble focusing and problem solving. One study found such children were at greater risk for leukemia. On the other side, some expectant mothers claim that smoking weed helped them avoid morning sickness.

149. A Performance Under-Enhancing Drug

If steroids make athletes like Roger Clemens or Manny Ramirez run faster or hit a baseball harder, grass seems to have the opposite effect. After all, it affects your reaction time, judgment, and perception. Not surprisingly, athletes who smoke grass find that their skills degenerate over time. It's also generally illegal to use marijuana before a contest. Snowboarder Ross Rebagliati lost his Olympic gold medal after officials determined he'd used grass within forty-eight hours before competing. His explanation, that he was around friends who used it, but he didn't inhale, didn't pass muster, and they stripped him of his honors.

150. And What about Jail Time?

It's true that there are many places where you can smoke weed more or less in safety—not that many people's homes are subject to marijuana raids—but that doesn't change the fact that smoking is still against the law. In 2007, cops busted more than 872,000 people for "marijuana violations" according to the National Organization for the Reform of Marijuana Laws (NORML). During the first eight years of the twenty-first century, nearly 9 million people were arrested for possession or dealing. So if someone tells you that you can't get busted for pot . . . they're smokin' something.

CHAPTER SEVEN

ganja survival guide

Hiding Your Stash

> Richard Vernon (Paul Gleason): What if your dope was on fire?
> John Bender (Judd Nelson): Impossible, sir . . . it's in Johnson's underwear.

> —*The Breakfast Club*

151. Maxwell House High

When you're looking for the perfect place to hide weed in your home, the kitchen offers numerous options. One of the most timeless of these is the coffee tin in your pantry. Those tins are not only designed to keep what's inside moist and airtight, but also the strong smell of the coffee grounds creates a wonderful camouflage. Now, every morning, as you prepare to put your favorite stimulant into your body to face the day, you can be reminded of the depressant you will use later to forget it!

152. Purina Pot Stash

Ahh, the joy of pets. That cute little pantry where your girlfriend, wife, or mother keeps all those cans of cat food and bags of treats serves as a most inconspicuous and unassuming hiding place for your stash. Not only does it already smell in there, but also chances are you will already find a bag of catnip in there some-where, serving as a perfect decoy to prying eyes. "Honey, I *love* Mittens. I decided to buy her a bag of catnip, that's all." Just be careful not to confuse the two.

153. The Deodorant Stick Trick

This is a favorite for someone traveling. You simply need to buy a new stick of deodorant, twist it up until it falls off the spindle, and cut off some of the bottom section. Now, voila! You have an inconspicuous container that nobody can inspect without touching your used pit perfume, and the smell of the deodorant will mask just about anything (you knew that already).

154. Wake and Bake

The mattress is the most classic hiding spot of them all. It recalls the glory days of your adolescence when the mattress was the perfect place to hide the dirty maga-zines and notes from school. It seems like such an obvious choice, but that's the beauty of it. You probably wouldn't actually think of it right there under your nose. "No way he's hiding his stash under the mattress. That's just juvenile." Plus, who is really going to walk into your bedroom and have the audacity to lift your mat-tress and see what's underneath? That's just something you don't do.

155. Your Socks (When They Are on Your Feet)

For the pothead on the go, hiding illegal substances like a bag of nugget in your pants pockets just won't do. For a pot smoker, this is why socks were invented.

Sure, you might have athlete's foot and sweat like a whore in church, but that's why you put it in a nice plastic bag, right? That area right under the arch of your foot makes for the most inconspicuous spot. In the end, you can have the last laugh, telling your buddies how they smoked your foot fungus *after* the fact. It's a win-win situation.

156. Your Fake Limb (A Niche Market)

While it really is quite tragic that you lost that arm in the great Guitar Hero disaster of '08, you need to look on the bright side. Not only is the prosthetic limb a great conversation piece, but it also has another great advantage. Just imagine the possible amount of weed one could fit in a hollow arm. What's more, in these politically correct times, what police officer would stop you and ask that you empty the contents of your removable limb? Plus, your stash would never be too far away.

157. Cargo in the Car

Car manufacturers this day and age are always exploring newer and greater possibilities. While they may never come out and admit it, one can't help but have a sneaking suspicion they are *trying* to create hiding spots for our illegal inclinations. Go search your car, and with a bit of patience you will surely find an accessory (center console, dome light, clock, etc.) that illogically pops out, revealing ample space behind it, and pops back in. "What, officer? Um, no, I don't know why my clock is upside down."

158. Your Dreadlocks . . .

. . . or your Afro, if that's your style. Some hairstyles are just made for storage. Next time you are in a pinch to stash some stash, simply slide your nugget into your dreadlock and nobody will be the wiser. Plus, you are a pothead, so naturally most people will assume you are a filthy hippie in the first place; they'll think you've just been rolling around on the ground and hugging trees, and never think twice about it.

159. Praise Jesus for Pot

It may be sacrilegious, and it may guarantee you have a seat waiting for you in hell, but let's just admit it, the Bible just makes sense as a place to hide weed; it's commonplace, unexpected, and presumes morality. Simply open it up, take an X-ACTO knife and carve out a hole through the center pages, insert stash, close, and return to shelf. Now, next time your Dad visits your apartment, he may see the Bible in your bookcase, nod and smile in approval, and never get why you snickered.

160. Cannabis Canisters

Film cameras may be on their way out, but that doesn't mean a 35mm film canister isn't still one of the best, most cost-efficient, and space-saving places to hide weed on the planet. On top of that, you would be hard-pressed to find a more effective one, either. Those little plastic tubes are both light proof *and* airtight. However, if you start smoking large quantities, you might need to invest in a photography degree to keep up.

Getting Away with Getting High

"I see you're smoking pot now! I'm so glad. I think using illegal psychotropic substances is a very positive example to set for our daughter."

—Carolyn Burnham, played by Annette Bening, in *American Beauty*

161. Hit the Road

Again, that pesky driving under the influence law rears its ugly head. But one of the best places to get lit without getting caught is in your car. When you've got your car windows open and you're cruising, there's no chance that anyone can smell the skunk weed coming from your whip. So next time you have someone breathing down your neck and you need to relax with the help of some THC, hit the road and take a hit. Aside from Amsterdam, it's the safest place to toke.

162. Get High Up High

If you're lucky enough to live somewhere with a flat roof, you already know where I'm going with this one. Far above suspicious cops and the watchful eyes of your parents, the roof of your house or apartment building (or, better yet, the roof of a friend's house) provides a safe haven for rolling one up and getting blitzed. Sure, there is the danger of getting *too* high and stumbling off the roof. But if you stay away from the edge and watch your step, you'll find the roof one of the best places to burn away an afternoon.

163. At the Carnival (Except If You're Afraid of Clowns)

Sure, there are lots of kids and police officers at carnivals, but there are also lots of carnies. These guys make even the most stoned guy around look straight-edge. With the acid-washed jeans, ripped concert T-shirts, and constant Marlboro smoking, carnies provide the ideal distraction, enabling you and some buddies to toke up before hitting the Zipper for the third time. The only problem is this: you do *not* want to geek out around carnies—you'll end up living in the carnie trailer park next to the Tilt-a-Whirl and fried dough stand . . . hmm, maybe that wouldn't be the worst thing.

164. At Your House
(An Immediate Plus Is Your Movement Is Minimal)

Getting high at home is a risky venture. However, if you don't have a car, it's a risk you'll have to take. The trick here is timing. Try when your family is engaged in some type of distracting activity. Also, make the most of what you have: open the windows, turn on the fan, and run the shower, or turn on some music to cover the sound of any coughs you can't keep in. Even with those precautions, only get high on the home turf when you absolutely have to. If you get nabbed by your parents, you'll lose your buzz—fast.

ganja survival guide   **83**

165. Natural Health Food Stores Aren't Only for Losing Munchy Pounds

Wherever you find crunchy hippies, you're bound to find weed. So drop by a place where hippies commune—an organic grocery store or camping store works best. Then, do your best to blend in, and get buzzed. Your best bet is to avoid catching the dreadlocked cashier's attention. If that doesn't work, though, wander over to the employee break room and offer to share a bit of your stash. Someone will definitely take you up on the offer—and your odds of getting caught pretty much disappear.

166. Jam Out with Your Gram Out

Let's imagine for second you're not going to a stoner-friendly jam band show where a rolling haze of weed smoke is expected, if not welcomed. If you want to be inconspicuous about your consumption (or just don't want to share with your rocking-out neighbor in the jam band scenario), follow these tips to get high in hiding. Tip #1: use a one-hitter—for those not in the know, a one-hitter is a small pipe that smokes one small pack at a time and is easily concealable. Tip #2: duck and smoke; chances are everyone else is standing, so if you squat and toke you likely won't be seen. Tip #3: eat pot brownies.

167. Parks and Recreational Drugs

The sun's out. There's not a cloud in the sky. It's a beautiful day. What do you do? Go outside and get high, of course. But seeing as how marijuana is not yet legal, playing puff-puff-pass in your local park is still a no-no. Therefore, you need to be discreet. Do *not* yell about how high you want to get. Do *not* bring your two-foot Roor. Do *not* offer up a hit to the elderly couple taking a stroll. Simply lie in the grass, discreetly pass around a spliff, and feel the earth rotate.

168. Workin' Nine to High

Here's some advice on how to avoid getting caught when you're blazed on the job: always seem like you're high. Even when you're not high, assume the traits of a typical pothead. People will just think you're an aloof, lazy space cadet. No one would ever think you're high *that* often. This way when you do sneak out at lunch to light up, you can come back to the office and seem perfectly normal. If you don't assume the space cadet persona, someone will sniff you out post-pot-break—not literally though; hopefully you're smart enough to go back in after spraying yourself down.

169. Sand, Surf, Stoned

For stoner surfers, toking up before taking to the surf is like having a cup of coffee before heading to the office for stoner surfers. And while Spicoli wannabes might be able to carelessly bake on the beach, you should probably take a few discretionary steps before lighting up on the sand. First of all, make sure you're not near any families or lifeguards. A whiff of weed is likely to attract the authorities and get you kicked out. Second, leave the bong at home. Instead, light up an inconspicuous joint or—even safer—a spliff. Third, cover up the smell. If your beach allows BBQs or bonfires, get that secondary smoke going.

170. Dorm Dazed

Woo! College! It's all about beers, bongs, and . . . yeah, that's about it. If you're going to get high in your room though, you need to take the proper precautions. First, build a spoof (take a toilet paper roll and fill it with dryer sheets). Next, jam a rolled towel into the opening at the foot of your door. Then, get a fan and face it so the smoke blows out the window. Make sure everyone in the cipher exhales through the spoof and directly into the fan. After the session, you should spray some air freshener or cologne (incense is such a giveaway) and wait a few minutes before opening the door.

Pot Pranks

"Don't 'uuugh' me, Greek boy! How is it, that your fucking stupid, soon to be dead friends thought they might be able to steal my cannabis, and then sell it back to me?"

—Rory Breaker, played by Vas Blackwood, in *Lock, Stock, and Two Smoking Barrels*

171. Oregano: The Oldest Trick in the Book

It happens to the best of us at some time or another—probably back in high school. Oregano looks like pot when it's dried and chopped, so most smoking suckers won't realize until they light up that what they've got could be bought in the herb aisle at Stop & Shop. Just in case you're curious (and you're willing to try anything to get a high), oregano won't offer you any euphoria. It'll just make you cough and look like a fool—oh, and you might develop a lingering taste that reminds you of your grandmother's Christmas lasagna.

172. Donate Pot Cookies for the Charity Bake Sale

Ever wonder what your fellow churchgoers (cough, cough) would act like if they were high? Well, please your pastor and his parishioners by baking some of your stash into the brownies you offer up for the Sunday bake sale. You will not only feel good by volunteering and serving the Lord, but also you'll never have so much fun in your Sunday's best. Sit back and watch as the choir croaks out convoluted choruses, the ushers forget where they left their baskets, and the sermon offers up more giggles than last night's *SNL* monologue.

173. Slip Some Stank into Chili for the Family BBQ

Do you feel a little guilty about poisoning the Lord's faithful with your juvenile antics? Share your stash with the ones you love at your next family barbecue. God is bound to forgive you since they've sinned in raising a stoner like you anyway. Offer to make up some of your world-famous chili and sprinkle in some special ingredients. Once you slow-cook your way to silly satisfaction, pack up your creation and carry it over to Big Uncle Bob's backyard. Serve up heaping, smoking hot bowls of your cheeba-chili and watch as the fun ensues.

174. Piss in a Bong

Have a friend who is a moocher? Teach the dude a serious lesson by peeing into your bong before he takes a hit. The trick is to keep him from noticing the unsavory urine. One way to do this is to take the first hit, pass it around, and when your stash-stealing slouch of a stoner gets up to use the bathroom, empty out the water and replace it with the contents of your bladder. When he returns, tell him he gets the first hit since you all took one while he was in the john. One big inhale and the leech will have learned his lesson.

175. Offer a Joint Filled with Pencil Shavings

How often do your friends question what's in the joint by the time you've already rolled it up? You're known for your quality weed, so why not switch it up and play a prank that is sure to singe a serious memory in your friend's brain? Wrap a joint with pencil shavings rather than the good stuff, and tell your ball-busting buddy that he can take the first hit. After that one big hit, your friend's eyebrows will burn right off his face. After you stop convulsing in laughter, tell him that was your way of inviting him on your annual road trip to Burning Man.

176. Replace "Herb Blend" with *Herb* Blend

Maybe you've already tried the cheeba in the chili trick and your favorite high hostess was your good old mom. Want to see her floating fancy again but don't know how to pull it off? Sneak into her kitchen and replace your dear mother's herb blend with a blend of your own. You can either add your pot flakes to the oregano, basil, and rosemary or you can dump the whole thing out and really spice things up. Next, ask Mom to make your favorite—spaghetti and meatballs. When you sit down for dinner, enjoy the meal and the mayhem.

177. Take Two, Tobacco in the Bong

Do you have one of those friends who always acts really high but you can tell he is just putting on a show? Play a little prank on Pinocchio and see how far he's willing to go for a lie. Chances are the dude has no idea what he's doing when it comes to smoking up anyway, so fill up your bong with tobacco—much like you would for a hooka. Pass the bongie and watch as he takes a major hit. Dude, biggest one ever. Those eyes kind of close, he sits back, and finally lets out a giant exhale of smoke. Wait until he's started with his studied stoner stories, then call him out on his tall tales.

178. Prank Call Someone and Pretend to Be a Weed Dealer

Want to get one of your buddies in trouble or just play a mean old joke on him? Call the house and wait until someone other than your pal answers the phone. It could be his girlfriend, wife, or his folks. When his loved-one offers to take a message, simply say something like "yeah, man, tell him Skinny Pete is looking for him and he owes me for last night's toke." Next time you see your pal (after he's out of the doghouse) inquire if he's heard from Skinny Pete because you're looking for another bag.

179. Prank Call a Weed Dealer and Pretend to Be the FBI

Are you friends with a dealer? Or pissed at a dealer and want a little payback? Give the guy a call and act like the nonlocal law enforcement. Every dealer is always a bit nervous about getting caught and if he thinks the feds have his digits, he'll freak the fuck out. Paranoia can be fun to watch, but just don't take it so far that your source no longer wants to sell. When he picks up, repeat the following: "Is this Mr. _____? This is the Federal Bureau of Investigation and we have a couple of questions for you. If you have the time, we can meet you at your office. We're aware it's on the corner of _____ and _____. How's 9 P.M.?" That should do the trick, except if he has caller ID.

180. Steal Your Parents' Doob

If you're still living at home and want to light up but don't have any goods, take a look in your parent's room. If you're lucky enough to find their stash, go ahead and take it. Think about it: it's the easiest steal you'll ever make. They'll know it was you, but they won't be able to punish you for it since they don't want their little baby knowing about their drug habits. Don't make too much of a habit of hacking from your folks though, just every once in a while. They're just doing their parental duty by providing for their kin.

CHAPTER EIGHT

the highs of being high

The Bonuses of Smoking Weed

"When you smoke the herb, it reveals you to yourself."

—Bob Marley, musician

181. Spark Up, Spark Creativity

Go on, follow that loopy dream-train of thought your brain is riding. Write the song that'll put you on par with Dave Matthews. Pen the story that channels Kerouac. Tie-dye a shirt, or macramé a "plant" holder. Paint a landscape. Sketch a portrait. Take notes of the sky changing color and write a poem that captures the beauty of it all. Choreograph a free-form circle dance. Design a beautiful, flowing dress. Or . . . spark another spliff, turn up the music, and just sink into the couch. There'll be time for creativity tomorrow.

182. It Makes Life More Bearable

Sick of your pain-in-the ass [insert any or all of the following that apply: boss, job, commute, coworkers, neighbors, parents, girlfriend, boyfriend, brother(s), sister(s), mail carrier, insurance agent, professor, friend, lover]? Need something to help you take the edge off as you deal with [insert any or all of the following that apply: your boss, your job, your commute, your coworkers, your neighbors, your parents, your girlfriend, your boyfriend, your brother(s), your sister(s), your mail carrier, your insurance agent, your professor, your friend, your lover]? Pack a bowl and smoke it. Weed makes it all a little easier.

183. Hair of the Dime Bag

If there was ever a time to wake and bake, this is it: when you're dragged out to a bachelor party with your high school buds and decide it's a good idea to down eight shots of whiskey in a span of three hours. This is especially true if your normal vibe is to kick back with some good weed. In which case, you'll wake up with one helluva hangover, cursing your friends and the feeble state of your pukey body. But getting agitated only makes matters worse, so stop, close your eyes, and fire up your bong. Because you know that with your first deep inhale of beautiful milky-white chronic the nausea will pass, the headache will fade, and the shakes will smooth out.

184. Toke Up, Get a Call from Judd Apatow

Okay, so even though the guy is antiweed—after all, Ben Stone (Seth Rogen) does quit smoking weed at the end of *Knocked Up*—Judd Apatow's work appeals deeply to the stoner sensibility. The comedic hotshots he works with is akin to a Who's Who list of Hollywood's best at "acting" high, including Rogen, Will Ferrell, Ben Stiller, Adam Sandler, Jack Black, Owen Wilson, Paul Rudd, James Franco, Jason Segel, John C. Reilly, Jonah Hill, and Danny McBride. If you keep on smoking and learn to adopt the mannerisms of Rogen, you could be well on your way to costarring in *Pineapple Express 2.*

185. Toke Up, Get a Call from Jennifer Aniston

Poor Jen. So misunderstood. Don't those nasty tabloid reporters know that having to work opposite David Schwimmer for what seems like decades would drive any red-blooded woman to the bowl? So she toked up now and again—big fucking deal. She found True Romance with Brad Pitt, and together they shared some truly high times. Then she took up with Dodgeballer Vince Vaughn (although they couldn't keep the good times rolling). Then, Mr. Wonderland, John Mayer, who was more concerned with the size of his schlong than the size of his bong. Needless to say, that didn't last. Could you be next?

186. Pothead Poker Face

According to an informal poll done by the folks at Pokerkingblog.com, many well-known live and online poker pros smoked marijuana—and smoked heavily. We're not just talking about a casual Saturday night toke here; these guys smoked before big tournaments, during the breaks of big tournaments, and after big tournaments.

Among other things, these players claimed pot helped their game by giving them increased sustenance. Makes sense. While stoned, you constantly seek out munchies. Compare this to a player who may spend hours playing without taking a break to eat—he's hungry and tired, with a malnourished brain. Score another victory for the stoners.

187. Reduce Your Carbon Footprint

"Going green is like smoking marijuana," Owen Wilson reportedly announced at a Live Earth eco-friendly weekend in Cali. No idea what that *really* means, but hey, partaking in a green bud like pot has got to put you squarely in the Prius-driving, plastic-bag-eschewing, Al Gore camp, jah? Marijuana is a plant, after all, and it can be grown in your very own yard (no black light necessary!) if you are a crafty gardener/harvester and can hide it from the fuzz. In any case, it *is* biodegradable, compostable, and smokable, leaving nothing behind but some resin in the bong water. Use that to nourish your new stash, and you'll be the greenest pothead on the block.

188. Mary Jane as Meds

Assuming you don't have the misfortune of suffering from one of the many ailments that medicinal marijuana can help alleviate, it would still behoove you to go to great lengths to get your hands on that magic card that allows you access to this primo bud. As a purely preventive measure, of course. For one, it's a lot cleaner to go through the state for your weed than through your sketchy hookup. Consider it a little slice of Amsterdam here in the states. You can toke up with a clean conscience knowing that you are doing your part to ward off glaucoma, MS, and minimize the affects of Tourette's and OCD.

189. Non-FDA-Approved Morning Sickness Relief

Suppose you're knocked up. And you're in your first trimester (for those of you who have no idea what the hell that is, it's the first three months of prego; rent *Knocked Up* for more info) and you're puking every goddamn morning. What's the harm in firing up the bong and allowing the queasiness to pass? Weed is proven to soothe an upset stomach, although your OB/GYN probably wouldn't condone this kind of "irresponsible" behavior. Honestly, what's the worse thing that can happen? Your bundle of joy will be a little mellower than other babies and might crave brownies instead of formula.

190. Red Wine + Pot = Young Mind

In a very awesome 2008 study by Ohio State University, researchers found a link between properties in red wine (polyphenols) and properties in pot (THC) that can work to keep your brain healthy and nimble as you age. While the experts in the study wouldn't go so far as to endorse marijuana to help ward off such diseases as Alzheimer's, they said that the psychoactive agent in cannabis can reduce inflammation in the brain and perhaps even stimulate growth of brain cells. So to the average pothead-hater, you might look like you're killing brain cells, but it's more likely that you're *repairing it* with every puff. Sweeeet.

The Stoner Bond

Harold Lee (John Cho): Yo, I'm not joining the mile high club with you!

Kumar Patel (Kal Penn): What about the really high club?

—*Harold & Kumar Escape from Guantanamo Bay*

191. Jimmy, the Janitor at Your School

When you were younger, the janitor at your school was just the creepy old guy you were sure went through your locker. As you became older, though, you began to feel like you had more in common with the custodian than any of your teachers. Before you knew it, you were sticking around after school to get lit in the janitor's closet. Think about it—would you ever have even spoken to the man who cleans up after you if you didn't smoke weed? Would you have known about the service elevator that gets you to the locker room in half the time than it used to take you if you didn't love getting high? So, next time you think about quitting, think about the friendship you formed with the janitor.

192. Wally, Your Friend's Weird Uncle

Life got a lot more interesting when you started getting high. And sometimes, weird people seem a lot less weird when you smoke a bowl with them. Take your friend's weird uncle. He used to be that strange dude who lived in your friend's basement, forever mooching off his sister's family. Now that you've gotten high together, you begin to realize he's not weird—he's cool! So before you judge an unemployed family friend, find out if he gets high. Adults will be much less suspicious since you're under adult supervision—leaving you to smoke all the weed you want.

193. Bruno, the Dickhead Bouncer

Is there anything worse than a meathead bouncer with a superiority complex? But sometimes, they're a package deal with a cool bar or club (complete with hot girls). What's a stoner to do? I think you know the answer to that question. Instead of offering twenty bucks to get in, tell the dickhead you can hook him up. Hopefully, he likes to get high. Before you know it, you're in. Sure, it may have cost you some dank, but a guy's gotta do what a guy's gotta do.

194. Mary, Your Best Friend's Mom
Warning: make sure your buddy's not around when you're reading this entry.

Having a friend with a hot mom is a blessing and a curse. You get to see her sun-bathing in the backyard, but you have the awkward situation of finding reasons to hang out with her without pissing off your friend. The win-win situation? Get high together. Assuming she's cool with pot smoking, no one gets in trouble here. You get to hang out with a MILF, and you all get a little red-eyed fun. Just be sure Stiffler's mom is into weed before you offer a joint. This would be a hard one to explain to your parents.

195. Band Camp Geeks
Sure, they're skinny, dorky, and they travel in packs. But band geeks are also musi-cians. And if there's one thing musicians like, it's, well, it's music. But the second thing is getting high. Before you write off these wind-instrument nerds as too nerdy to chill with, try offering a friendly joint to one of these artists. They'll prob-ably not only accept, but also turn you on to a better kind of weed. Hey, they're not doing it for the uniforms.

196. Norm, Your NORML Rep

So you've never been a big fan of politics. But you are a big fan of weed. And if there's any chance that pot is ever going to be legalized, the National Organization for the Reform of Marijuana Laws will be the peeps that get it done. If you love cannabis enough to fight for your (and fellow pot lovers') weed-smoking rights, visit *www.norml.org* to find your local chapter. You may find yourself working side-by-side with an eighty-year-old life-long pot smoker, or a cute chick you've never met before. Either way, you're sure to meet some interesting and friendly people working for a good cause. If nothing else, you know it will be a mellow group.

197. Laura, the Way, Way, Way Out of Your League Chick

She's funny, hot, and has a smokin' body. You're dorky, not hot, and like to put smoke in your body. One way you may have a shot? Offer to get her high. Through the pleasant fog of a good buzz, your geekiness now makes you seem intelligent. Your slacker attitude? You're just free-spirited. Proceed with caution on this one, though—if she doesn't like weed, she may just think you're more of a loser than she already does.

198. Clyde, the Clerk at 7-11

You're young, unemployed, and sometimes lazy. He's older and a hard worker. Yet due to the amount of weed you smoke (which leads to a lot of Funyun and candy consumption), you seem to spend a lot of time at 7-11. At first, your regular visits to his store pissed him off. Now that he's gotten to know you, he's figured out you're not going to steal anything—you can pay for your Twinkies just like a nonstoner can. True, your relationship may be mostly financial, but once again, it's a friendship that never would have happened without weed.

199. The Band Playing Your City

After a concert, don't be that guy hanging out near the venue, begging the headliners to autograph your T-shirt. Odds are, they'll blow right by you. But if you offer the band a toke, don't be surprised when you find yourself smoking up backstage. Your friends will be jealous, you'll have awesome pictures for your Facebook page, and odds are, they have even better weed to share.

200. Eddie Lee, the Chinese Food Delivery Guy

How many times have you made this guy come out in the rain or late at night to give you a crab Rangoon fix? The least you can do is get the guy high. The next time you get a jonesing for take-out, roll up a joint for the delivery guy. Don't give him weed in place of a tip—after all, the guy is working for a living. Rather, think of it as a little bonus. Added bonus? Next time you order dinner, you can guarantee it will arrive much faster than usual.

Other Uses for Cannabis

"Carrots! Medicinal carrots! Personal use medicinal carrots that were here when I moved in and I'm holding it for a friend!"

—Stephen, played by Alan Tudyk, on *Dollhouse*

201. Take Two Pills and Call Me in the Morning

Medicinal marijuana has become the herbal therapy prescription for many people experiencing pain—whether it's from side effects of cancer treatments, surgery recoveries, or chronic pain conditions. So the question here is if doctors prescribe pot as medicine, how can it be so "bad" for you? The truth is doctors prescribe THC pills—not joints, bongs, and pot brownies. Sorry to rain on your smoke parade, but medicinal cannabis is a serious matter and unfortunately you have to be really sick to get your pharmacist to act as your dealer and exchange some cheeba simply for a co-pay.

202. Wearing Your Weed

The word *cannabis* comes from the botanical family name Cannabaceae, and it is also the genus name of a group of annual flowering plants more commonly known as *hemp* plants. You've probably heard that hemp clothes are out there, but have you ever actually seen someone sporting the ganja? Say you're dating a girl and you find out she's wearing a hemp dress. Is a part of you just a little curious how that dress will light up and smoke? Well, sorry to break it to you but Burning Woman ain't gonna get you high. Hemp plants are cultivated for commercial uses rather than drug use, so save the tailoring for the seamstress.

203. Fuel Up!

While you might think it's crazy to run your car on cannabis—what a waste!—some people think we should. Hemp plants act much like corn and waste paper when it comes to biomass, which we all know is the term of the times. We've got to stop burning through the ozone and if using pot plants helps us save the earth and all of the earthlings, how can it still be illegal? That's what you should say to the cops if they ever catch you growing the grass. You're saving the earth, man.

204. Fiber Me This . . .

Ever wish you lived in Colonial times? Things were so much easier back then. We might think settlers were lucky not to have text messages, the stock market, and Britney Spears to deal with, but they also didn't have Metamucil or Fiber One bars. So how did they keep healthy enough to grow the Union? You guessed it, hemp. Cultivating ganja crop for nutritional purposes dates back more than 10,000 years and it's only obvious that our brilliant founding fathers partook in the pot plot. After a while, all those potatoes were bound to catch up with them, so before they pledged allegiance to the flag, Colonial dudes embraced the cheeba.

205. Let the Pooch Play

You can't leave your canine companion out of the ganja-loving gang. Hemp collars, dog beds, and canine clothing (although you would never do that, would you?) are widely available. Much like hemp clothing for humans, pet supplies made of pot are said to be durable and sustainable. So if your pooch lunges after your pot brownies or his tail's about to knock the bong off its perch, yank on that hemp leash and keep your animal in order. Both you and your greedy, pot-stealing moochers will be thankful for the hardiness of the hemp.

206. Lay the Foundation with "Hempcrete"

Next time you are building yourself a basketball court or (more likely) repaving the driveway, choose the environment-friendly alternative to concrete—hempcrete. You don't have to be a total stoner to see the advantage of using hempcrete. In fact, sober or not, you'll be surprised how effective the stuff is. Those who have used hempcrete say that it's not only better for our earth, but also more durable than concrete. Apparently when considering the cretes head-to-head, the one made with our favorite plant is stronger, doesn't crack as much, and weighs about half as much—which comes in handy when your dad asks you to haul in the load from the car.

207. Stay Hydrated with Hemp

You've already learned that hemp has been used for nutritional purposes such as fiber, but according to health experts in Britain, hemp seeds are also a good source of protein. Containing essential amino acids, the oil in hemp seed can be considered important for maintenance of a healthy body. So—with you and your health in mind—certain restaurants in Europe offer up hemp lager, hemp iced-tea, hemp coffee, and hemp tea. And since some people go so far as to call hemp a "vegetable," you can use it in your Nutritional Pyramid.

208. Dope Rope

Although it's impossible to mark exactly when hemp was first used to make rope, historians estimate early man wove hemp ropes and fastened bamboo together to make floating rafts—so, yeah, that's a long time ago. Before all of the synthetic stuff that we use today was created, rafts, pulleys, and fishnets were likely all fashioned from hemp seed. If you're interested in learning more about the history of hemp rope, you can find information in local and national maritime museums. Smoke a joint and join the museum tour; those museum tour guides will never seem so cool.

209. Homemade, with Hempseed

Hempseed can be included as an ingredient in any number of foods. While most people think of pot brownies when they think about reefer food, broaden your horizons and try your stash in any course, any time. Start off with baked goods, then experiment with full entrées, then share your yummy, giggle-inducing creations with your friends and family. Also, the Food Network doesn't have a hempseed show yet, so this might be your shot at stardom.

210. Pot Paper—Then and Now

Some people say that Benjamin Franklin owned a hemp paper mill—and others go so far as to say the actual Declaration of Independence was drafted on hemp paper! Seriously, those Colonial folk were cool cats. Whether you believe these theories about our Founding Fathers or not, hemp paper is still around today and thus we need to consider how to use pot paper in our current lives. Forget all-natural stationery and recyclable schoolbooks: roll up your best roach with some hemp sheet and write your own history (seriously, write it down 'cause you might forget it).

CHAPTER NINE

*this is you on drugs . . .
any questions?*

How to Tell If You're High

"When you're high, you can do everything you normally do, just as well. You just realize that it's not worth the fucking effort. There is a difference."

—Bill Hicks, standup comedian

211. You Just Polished Off a Jar of Pickle Juice

You may not want to admit it, but we've all eaten some gnarly things while high. Whether it's chasing two Crunch Wraps from Taco Bell with a mint chocolate Blizzard from DQ or covering still-frozen corn with ranch dressing, everything tastes better when you're ripped. And since you're stone, you're probably too lazy to actually cook anything. So if the twenty-five kosher dill spears haven't satisfied your appetite, knock back the juice, too—just be prepared to spend some time on the crapper.

212. For the Last Ten Minutes, You've Been Repeating the Same Word

You just burned a joint and now you're watching *Superbad* for what seems like the millionth time. Looking to switch it up, your friend asks you for the remote. How is it that you never noticed how funny the word *remote* is? You know how the next five to sixty minutes go: you repeat the word over and over until it loses its meaning, finding a humorous aspect with every "moooote." Sure, it's dumb, but you can't help where comedy genius strikes—especially when you've been smoking all day. So next time you're high, pay attention to all the absurd and goofy-sounding words that come up—it's unintentional comedy at its highest.

213. Your Face Is Tingling

The Man may bitch about how weed affects your reaction time and numbs your senses, but the Man obviously never got high. If he did, he would surely realize that pot actually heightens your senses. How else can you explain the tingly feeling that takes over your face, hands, and every other part of your body when you smoke some especially dank weed? So if you just smoked up and it feels like tiny bugs are crawling on you, don't panic. Just sit back, pack another bowl, and try to enjoy (or at least not wig out over) the sensation of feeling your blood course through your very stoned veins.

214. You Can Actually Tolerate Jam Bands

You've been listening to Trey Anastasio noodle for the last twenty minutes and you're still entertained, so guess what? You're high. There's a reason that only stoners can tolerate jam bands. Songs need choruses, vocals, a beat—if you're not high. Guitar solos are great, but if you find yourself dancing after the thirty-minute mark on a Phish (or String Cheese Incident, G. Love, or whomever else) song, you know you're high. If you just burned one, though, and "Bouncin' Round the Room" is still keeping your attention, turn up the volume—and enjoy what *must* be a really good high.

215. You Slept for More than Fifteen Consecutive Hours

Sure, a quick roach can get your blood pumping in the morning. But if your wake and bake is followed up with bong rips and a couple pot cookies, odds are, you'll need a nap sometime today. The amazing thing about weed-induced sleeps is the uncanny ability to sleep for hours on end. So if you're cool with missing most daylight hours, why not lie down for a pot-inspired sleep? Not only are you guaranteed to get two nights of sleep in one fell swoop, but you'll also have some pretty funky dreams.

216. You're Actually Laughing at Crappy Shows Like *Gary, Unmarried*

If you're flipping through the channels and find yourself stopping at one of those bullshit fat-guy-with-unreasonably-hot-wife sitcoms (think Kevin James), jackpot! You're high. The bad news is that you're actually making yourself dumber. The good news? You're actually making yourself dumber, so you can tolerate mindless sitcom plots. So sit back, relax, and enjoy the canned laugh track. If you start finding yourself underwhelmed, change the channel—or twist up another J and keep on laughing.

217. You're Driving Sixteen Miles per Hour (On the Highway)

Technically you're not supposed to drive while high. But anyone who has tested this law knows you don't have to worry about speeding. Who knows what it is about being high behind the wheel that makes you drive so slowly—the paranoia of being pulled over, the distraction of a jam band's sounds coming through the speakers, or the numbing of senses—but you're much more likely to travel under the speed limit when high. So if you find yourself going twenty miles per hour in the left-hand lane, do yourself and everyone else on the road with somewhere to go a favor: pull over and take a nap.

218. Your Own Bad Poetry Is Making You Cry

You're not the first stoner to put the pen to the paper when under the influence of some high-quality THC—and you won't be the last. But don't let that deter your creative process. Throw on a beret, put on some Flemish flute music, and let your creative juices flow. Whether you're writing about teenage angst, your childhood pet cocker spaniel (now dead), or the plight of the hungry, don't be surprised if the combination of emotions and pot gets the tears flowing. But hey, man, no need to be embarrassed. You're an artist. A stoned artist.

219. You Don't Remember a Time When You Didn't Cough

The sad irony of really good weed is that the better the pot, the more you cough. Coughing is a blessing and a curse, though. While it's annoying and will certainly blow your cover, there's nothing like a good cough to take you from "kind of buzzed" to "face down." So whether you're choking down a quick spliff or taking bong rips, a good cough will get you where you want to be. Unfortunately, the cough lasts as long as the high does.

220. You Take Absurdly Long Detours . . .

. . . just to avoid driving by the police station. Sure, you know that cops can't actually tell you're high just by looking at your car, but you're not taking any chances. So on your way to In-N-Out Burger, you go across town, get on the highway, and before you know it your ten-minute burger run has become an hour-long, across-town trek. Sure, your mom may wonder what the hell took you so long, but you don't have to waste any time (or brain cells) worrying about the Man sniffing out you—or your weed.

Smoke Your Paranoia Away

"Last week, Dwight found half a joint in the parking lot. And as it turns out, Dwight finding drugs is scarier than most people using drugs."

—Jim Halpert, played by John Krasinski, in *The Office*

221. Being Killed

Even if you're in the safety of your basement or living room, you still get the paranoid feeling that everybody wants you dead for one irrational reason or another. When you are in this situation, you don't have many options that don't involve being scared of everybody around you. However, if you are the friend of this "murder victim," your empathy will soon transgress to apathy after the "murder victim" starts ruining your own buzz with the negative vibes. The only solution is to smoke until you and your friend are allies against those deadly assassins.

222. Parents Catching You Smoking

You've worked so hard to make sure your parents think you're a model citizen. However, they could come home early at any point and find you and your friends high off your asses and staring at a lava lamp. What to do? You must be in a well-ventilated room, with air spray handy (using whiskey and/or beer to cover up the smell is only adding to your problems); you have to have places to hide weed and pipes (see Chapter 7); and your friends need to have an escape route (suggestion: run into the woods in the backyard).

223. Medical Conditions

While you're stoned, all of a sudden every medical condition that you have comes to the forefront of your concerns. It doesn't matter if you have diabetes or ADD, you are convinced that it might just kill you, and none of your friends are competent at that very moment to help you. You try to concentrate on everything that can prevent your symptoms to overcompensate for your paranoia that weed will automatically cause your medical condition. This makes it even worse. However, you can keep your medication nearby and, more than likely, there is a study out there that says pot cures your illness anyway (Wikipedia counts as a source if you're high).

224. Time Warp

You've been smoking the whole afternoon and all of a sudden someone starts talking to you in slow motion. Wait, does this weed that you've been smoking control time and space? Have you somehow broken the time barrier and are able to control how fast people talk? How much time has passed anyway? These questions might make you paranoid about how much power you hold, but chillax, and offer the person who is talking in slow motion more weed until she speaks at a normal speed. Whatever you do, you shouldn't watch the beginning of *Lost*, season five, while this slow motion is happening—your mind might actually explode.

225. Running Out of Food

You have smoked a nice bowl, and, as you start eating that bag of Doritos, you suddenly think, what if this is the last bag of Doritos in your possession? You never want the feeling of being so hungry that your friends look like large hamburgers with hot dogs for legs and nachos for arms. Next time, you should plan ahead and stock up on all of the essential munchies (see Chapter 2). You just don't want to get out of control to the point where you're spending more on junk food than weed.

226. Everyone Knows You're High

Sure, among your friends when you're passing around a pipe, you don't really care if any of them knows you're high. However, occasionally while you're high, you have to venture out into the outside world to grab snacks. All of a sudden, everybody seems like they know you're high and, at any moment, will call the cops on you. The more time you spend around them, the worse your paranoia becomes. Unless you went to high school with the cops in the town and the only thing they would do is laugh at you, you should create a designated snack-getter and stay inside.

227. The Weed Is Laced with a Hallucinogenic Drug

You've just smoked a bowl and it's really hit you . . . *really* hit you, as in, you question if you have ever been higher before. Do you remember that scene in *Empire Records* when Mark eats those brownies and Gwar starts talking to him and feeds him to the worm? Yeah, it's like that. If your weed is actually laced, you have at least learned which dealer you shouldn't buy from, or which friend's weed to avoid. If the cannabis is not laced though, you have an obligation to suck it up and smoke more.

228. Going to Be High Forever

You've been enjoying your high for a while, and it's cool and all, but then you think to yourself, "Wait, this isn't going to last forever, right?" Then your brain runs a stream of consciousness of all the times that you don't want to be high, from taking school exams to visiting your parents. Unlike when you were laughing before at everything, you're now laughing out of hysteria. You need to take a page out of *The Hitchhiker's Guide to the Galaxy* and *don't panic*—you can find something shiny and let that amuse you until you come down.

229. Cops

Perhaps, you remember the DARE class when that cop who taught the class had it out for you. Or maybe you just watched a marathon of *Cops*. Whatever the case, you have developed both a serious paranoia about smoking cannabis and a resentment of the men in blue. On the one hand, you want to smoke to revolt against the police. On the other hand, officers have instilled a fear in you that they could crash through the wall like Punchy, the Hawaiian Punch mascot, and bust you at any moment. Of course, you should choose smoking, but just make sure you don't rebel openly against the police (they don't take kindly to that).

230. Flashing Lights (Especially If They're Blue)

Flashing lights cause both paranoia and frightening trips. If you are tripping and someone messes with you by putting a strobe light on, you'll probably become paranoid about any of the other subjects (especially being killed) in this section. Also, remember the entry about being paranoid about a medical condition? If you have a history of seizures and there are flashing lights, you're actually justified to be paranoid. If your friends have blue lights that turn on in their apartment or car, you are to disown them until they recover from being douche bags.

CHAPTER TEN

STONER UTOPIA

Stoner Equals Humanitarian

"You know, sometimes I wish I did a little more with my life instead of hangin' out in front of places sellin' weed and shit. Like, maybe be an animal doctor. Why not me? I like seals and shit."

—Jay, played by Jason Mewes, in *Clerks II*

231. Rid the World of Horrible Corporate Rock

'30s Jazz, and '60s folk and rock music movements also had ties to weed, and hip-hop has entire songs, albums, and artists (hi, Cypress Hill) dedicated to it. The time is ripe for a musical renaissance where the Britneys, Christinas, and American Idol winners of the world would fade to the Jimis, Phishs, and Ice Cubes. Close the garage door, jam it with a towel, and get going!

232. The Munchies Are Actually Helpful

Pot can help those suffering in the late stages of cancer and AIDS by giving them the desire to eat. Glaucoma patients extol the virtues of marijuana. If you and your pothead brethren were able to get involved with outpatient treatment, all of you could provide not only weed but also much-needed company and support for patients. Also, hospitals are great sources of weird shit to make into bongs. However, you and your stoner pals should think twice about fishbowling in the surgical ward.

233. Can't We All Just Get Along?

If you and your pothead friends ran things, marijuana would be abundant and the Mexican cartels that have been murdering each other (and innocent civilians) by the thousands would be a thing of the past. They could put down the AK and pick up the pipe. Mexico has always been at the forefront of ganja smoking, and a new wave of good will (helped along by a new wave of good bud) could give our neighbors down south a bit of peace. If the plantations were overseen by an empowered Mexican government, conditions for growing weed would be better too.

234. Smokin' Economic Stimulus

Forget the military industrial complex—potheads could solve the economic crisis through the marijuana industrial complex. Not only would they be on the ground floor to a burgeoning industry, but also people who were on the fence or otherwise kept out of drug dealing for fear of arrest or consorting with seedy folk might find new opportunities as the forklift drivers, lawyers, and secretaries of Pot Co. or Ganja Inc. Subindustries would also crop up, if you'll excuse the pun—thus begins the race to build a better bong.

235. Take That, Al Gore

What's a better way to counteract global warming than planting a shitload of plants? Granted, some of this may be offset by the emissions made by smoking the plants, but new green initiatives could encourage people to responsibly bake their stash into brownies or pound cakes. A populace of potheads would drive less often as well, reducing CO_2 emissions. And you could turn down the heat in the winter because you'd already be nice and toasty.

236. Change We Can Believe In

Americans have become more and more on edge lately. There's a deep divide between right and left, and increasingly, Americans feel an incredible sense of entitlement. They need to follow your lead, take a step back, and toke up. If everyone got stoned and just sat for a minute, they'd see the guy across the table and think, "You know what, he's just like me." We're all sharing the deep inhaling of life together, and it's important not to hold onto the material things. Like that pipe. Remember: puff, puff, pass.

237. Going Dutch

You and your stoner comrades would do away with DARE and bring in DUTCH (Do Use The Crazy Hashish). Holland has decriminalized weed and rates of use are lower than that of the United States. Portugal, too, decriminalized cannabis, and saw its rates of teenage drug use drop. Rather than treat their population as children to be punished, both countries accepted and subsequently lowered the risks involved with pot use by letting people make up their own minds. Potheads would do the same.

238. Detroit Pot City

Can you say "hotbox"? Stoners would not only carpool far more often—part of the conservational spirit behind fishbowling—but also potheads would naturally make the best car designers too. The Volkswagen Beetle, the Volvo 240, the Cutlass Supreme—all of these are classic cars, and none of them are in production any-more. No wonder nobody's buying! If it's not a ridiculously slow electrical fire wait-ing to happen, Swedish, or a floating couch, what's the point?

239. Feed the World . . . with Twinkies

Nothing would ramp up world food production like a nation of stoners. And what would be done with the excess Twinkies, MoonPies, and large milkshakes left over? They would be airlifted to nations in need, that's what. And since those nations could be revitalized and put to work growing entire fields of ganja, this would cause impoverished third world countries to gain valuable resources to trade and make a profit. You know who would be a good trade partner? The new United States of Stoners.

240. Potheads Don't Know Left from Right

There are a great many problems that plague the United States, but none of them are more dangerous than the political rift between right and left. If stoners were in charge, there would be no right or left. There would be one vast Philosopher's Party, and everyone would think everyone else's ideas are actually pretty cool, if you think about it. What makes people consider the other side more than smoking a bowl together and discussing it for three hours over some chips?

Sanctioned Smoking

"Look, Lois, ever since marijuana was legalized, crime has gone down, productivity is up, and ratings for *Doctor Who* are through the roof."

—Brian Griffin, voiced by Seth MacFarlane, on *Family Guy*

241. The Burning Man Model

Throughout history, marijuana has brought people together. Virtually the entire jazz community of the 1930s smoked pot. The antiwar movement was partially run by people who were high much of the time. Since the mid-'80s, the Burning Man festival has allowed people the opportunity to come together, generally get stoned, and to weld together giant bikes. In the modern era of television, video games, and increased isolation from the rest of humanity, legalizing weed would bring you together with the rest of the world, if only to organize runs to pizza joints.

242. Smoke Local

According to the *New York Times*, law enforcement officials reported that around 60 percent of illegal drugs—marijuana being a main one—arrives through the border of Arizona and Mexico. Also, according to a 2008 Congressional report, this illegal importing caused violent confrontations with traffickers, resulting in more than 6,000 deaths, including hundreds of cops, in 2008. If you and your cohorts helped legalize marijuana, it would stop the demand for importing weed and diminish the violence. Also, this is a win-win situation for border police: they would be in less danger because of the decrease in drug violence, *and* after a long day patrolling the border, they could relax with some nice domestic weed.

243. Uncle Smokin' Sam

You not only would be able to make more money, but also Uncle Sam would get his grubby fingers in on the act too. By taxing pot sales, America could further pay off its national debt, build high-speed rail systems, or buy several of those new stealth fighters that other countries envy. Part of the profits could further go into education and rehabilitation for people who are hooked on actual, problematic drugs. Also, those potholes on Main Street would get filled in, using proceeds from the 5 percent tax on all the pot and doughnut holes you buy.

244. Think of the Children!

No, seriously. Because pot is sold illegally and left unregulated, it's as easy for kids to get ahold of as it is for adults. Making pot legal under similar age restrictions as cigarettes would make it more difficult for kids to get blazed before school. It wouldn't be impossible to obtain—you can still get a less ethical adult to buy alcohol or cigarettes when you're underage—but it might give the DARE officer something to do with the extra time he has now that pot is off the curriculum.

245. Ending Pot Prejudice

Many of the arguments against marijuana come from racial sentiment. The word itself came into popular use because it sounded more "Mexican," and Americans in the '30s were expected to hate it for that reason alone. If pot were legalized, one less tool would be usable against minorities, who have higher rates of arrest and conviction compared to their white brethren regarding marijuana possession convictions. Smoking weed would unite people of different races rather than alienate them from each other.

246. Stoners Released from the Slammer

By the same token, prison populations would drop dramatically. Of the 872,720 people incarcerated for marijuana convictions, 775,137 were for possession. These people would be able to go back to their lives. Not only would this end the injustice of such ridiculous incarcerations, but it would also result in the possibility of closing more prisons as jail populations decrease. Legalization would drop entire categories of "crimes", and more violent crimes linked to profit motives would also decrease. Also, you wouldn't have to be paranoid about a cop busting you for an ounce of marijuana.

247. Make Love, Not War

Stoners can get pretty abstract themselves, but get this: back in 1969, President Nixon started the War on Drugs, taking the lead from President Dwight Eisenhower's War on Poverty. Since then, we've had all kinds of "Wars" on things—you might recall a recent War on Terrorism that has had similar results as the other Wars on Things. If marijuana is legalized, it will be the first step toward ceasing this ridiculous premise that declaring wars on words will solve anything.

248. Rastafarians Go Mainstream

Rastafarians have long been restricted to Jamaica and college dorm rooms. Allowing the most recognizable aspect of Rastafarianism to be legal in the United States will let you and your pot-loving friends celebrate religious rituals without isolation. The Virgin Mary's image is "seen" and worshiped on a grilled cheese sandwich, so other religious followers shouldn't be denied their more effective methods of showing spirituality. And once Rastafarianism hits the mainstream, bobsledding will become the most popular sport in the world.

249. Potheads Against Drunk Drivers

You and almost every pot smoker you know smokes pot to escape. This reasoning is shared with alcohol, pot's liquid cousin. While it is also used for escapism, it is not as addictive as alcohol, nor is it as detrimental in terms of violence caused while under the influence. If pot were made legal, it stands to reason people would drink less and get high more. Fewer drunks equals fewer drunk drivers and drunk-driving accidents.

250. Let the Cops Eat More Donuts

Nothing ruins your buzz like the boys in blue. While the police serve a legitimate function in controlling unlawful situations and preventing crimes from happening, they also waste a great deal of time and money trying to catch people for smoking pot. If pot is legalized, the police will have more time to spend doing other things, like setting up traffic stops or ticketing your car. Okay, so this may not actually resolve much, but at least you wouldn't get tossed in jail over a bag of skunk weed, and that's the real point of legalization.

CHAPTER ELEVEN

the weed facts that will
freak you out

Smoking Out the Myths

"Well, Stan, the truth is marijuana probably isn't gonna make you kill people, and . . . it most likely isn't gonna fund terrorism, but . . . well son, pot makes you feel fine with being bored and . . . it's when you're bored that you should be learning some new skill or discovering some new science or . . . being creative. If you smoke pot you may grow up to find out that you aren't good at anything!"

—Randy Marsh, voiced by Trey Parker, on *South Park*

251. Marijuana Is Dangerous

Antimarijuana activists often cite the dangers of weed as one of the top reasons that it should remain illegal. In 1972, the National Commission on Marihuana and Drug Use concluded that the dangers associated with smoking weed had been "grossly overstated." In 1995, the British medical journal *Lancet* said, "the smoking of cannabis, even long term, is not harmful to health." Marijuana does contain suspected carcinogens and particles that can irritate the lungs, but tobacco contains more. Further, marijuana smokers don't imbibe as often as cigarette smokers, so they inhale fewer of the potentially harmful particles.

252. Marijuana Causes Permanent Psychological Impairment

Marijuana makes you high. If this is news to you, you should turn in your rolling papers, your bong, and whatever other marijuana paraphernalia you have apparently been using incorrectly. Side effects are fewer and less scary than they are for Viagra, but they may include short-term memory loss, anxiety, and paranoia. However, there is no evidence that there are any lasting psychological effects—for adolescents or adults. Long-term memory is not affected, and there is no scientific evidence that marijuana use leads to mental illness. It does not diminish peoples' intellectual abilities or ambition. Behavior is not affected, and the short-term side effects of marijuana use wear off and are only temporary.

253. Legalizing Marijuana Would Lead to More Auto Accidents

Legalizing marijuana does not mean that you would be allowed to smoke up and hit the road. Consuming high amounts of marijuana does impair visual perception and motor skills, but there is no scientific evidence to prove that it is any more harmful than alcohol or legal medications. Marijuana also tends to make drivers less likely to take risks on the road; alcohol increases risky behavior. Making it legal to carry and consume marijuana would not mean stoners would wreak havoc on the roads; legislation regarding operating motor vehicles and using marijuana would set parameters and keep everyone safe.

254. Hemp and Marijuana Are the Same

Hemp and marijuana are two different varieties of the cannabis plant, but they are by no means identical. Hemp can be used for industrial and commercial purposes, such as making fabric for clothing. It does not contain THC, the chemical in marijuana responsible for making you feel high, so smoking it won't do you a whole lot of good. In fact, industrial hemp actually contains a chemical that inhibits that high. Even so, growing hemp is not permitted in the United States even though it is an environment-friendly crop that is gaining market share in the clothing industry. You are allowed to sell and purchase products made with hemp, but the hemp has to be grown in other countries.

255. Marijuana Has No Medicinal Benefits

First, you should be aware of one thing: modern society can't take credit for discovering marijuana's medical uses. Marijuana has been used to treat various medical conditions for thousands of years. Medical professionals are becoming more vocal about the benefits of using marijuana for medical purposes. Marijuana can help many patients counteract the effects of their medical conditions or their treatments. For example, it stimulates the appetite, so it can help HIV patients keep their weight up and stay healthy longer. Marijuana's primary active ingredient is already used to make the synthetic drug, but nothing beats the real thing. Thirty-six states allow the use of marijuana for medical reasons, but federal law still prohibits it.

256. Marijuana Is More Potent Today than in the Past

In a word, no. For the most potent marijuana, you'd have to jump in your time machine and go back to the 1920s and 1930s. Smith-Klein, a pharmaceutical company, used to sell—legally—a product called "American Cannabis." The reason so many people are misinformed about the potency of modern marijuana has to do with faulty evidence. The claim that marijuana used to be less potent has its root in tests that were done on marijuana that was seized in the 1970s. This marijuana was not properly stored, and it degraded fairly rapidly. Because of this inaccurate testing, marijuana today does seem to have more THC in it. However, the reality is that today's weed is on par with the pot your parents smoked in the '70s.

257. The Marijuana Policy in the Netherlands Hasn't Worked

In short, if you're an adult over the age of eighteen in the Netherlands, you can purchase, possess, and consume marijuana. Shockingly enough, Dutch adults did not flock to the coffee shops to smoke up once marijuana was decriminalized. Nor did they become a nation of slackers and criminals. Rates of marijuana usage in the Netherlands are comparable to rates in the United States, although fewer Dutch adolescents light up. The Dutch government has no intention to reverse its stance on decriminalization; the law will remain much the same as it has for the last twenty years. Instead of wasting millions of dollars on fighting marijuana use, the Dutch government regulates and taxes the sale of weed and actually makes money off of it.

258. Antimarijuana Propaganda Works

As you know, if people want to smoke, they will do so. No amount of television advertising will convince them otherwise. The availability of marijuana in the

United States and many other parts of the world proves that the legalization of cannabis has a wide range of support. American society focuses on abstinence only (and, yes, we're still talking about weed here), but there is no evidence to suggest that antimarijuana propaganda or school programs that discourage the use of pot are effective. Studies show that marijuana use among adolescents rose in the 1990s, despite a renewed push for more antimarijuana programs.

259. Marijuana Use Makes You Lazy

Have you ever heard of Michael Phelps? He was a remarkably unmotivated fellow, wasn't he? We don't mean to imply that Phelps is a bona fide pothead. Also, the photos that showed his proficiency with a bong were snapped post-Beijing. However, the point stands. The guy isn't going to sink to the bottom of the pool just because he took a couple of hits. There is no scientific evidence to show that marijuana sucks the ambition out of someone who imbibes from time to time. So stick that in your pipe and smoke it.

260. Marijuana Kills Brain Cells

There is no reputable scientific evidence to support this claim. It's based on a poorly conducted study that was performed with rhesus monkeys in the 1970s. That flawed study claimed that it found prolonged exposure to marijuana smoke significantly altered the monkeys' brain structure in as few as six months. However, further studies have been unable to replicate these effects, so it's a pretty safe bet your brain cells are safe.

THC Trivia

"Is marijuana addictive? Yes, in the sense that most of the really pleasant things in life are worth endlessly repeating."

—Richard Neville, Australian writer

261. You Can Be Pious by Smoking Weed!

Though many devoutly religious men and women deny that pot had a place in the Bible, an alternative etymological theory presented by workers at the Hebrew University in Jerusalem says otherwise. They say that the word *cannabis* actually comes from the Arabic "kunnab," which comes from the Syric "qunnappa," which came from the Hebrew "pannag." They say that this explains that the "pannag" that Ezekiel mentions in the Bible (27:17) would therefore be cannabis. "Reed of balm" in the bible (*kan bosm*) is also thought to translate to cannabis, as it is rendered in traditional Hebrew as "kannabos" or "kannabus."

262. And You Thought You Had It Bad in America

In the Philippines, the penalty for possessing 500 grams (almost a pound) of marijuana is the death penalty. Under the Comprehensive Dangerous Drugs Act of 2002 that President Gloria Macapagal-Arroyo signed into law, drug dealing in any quantity and possession of 10 grams of opium, morphine, heroin, ecstasy, or cocaine are also offenses punishable by death. Having more than 5 grams of any hard drug warrants life in prison, and a possession of any amount up to 5 grams will get you twelve years in prison. Those Filipinos don't mess around.

263. If This Happened Every Time, You Would Want America Always to Be at War

During World War II, the American government actually requested that more people grow hemp. The country's supply of hemp boat rigging and canvas, which normally came from the South Pacific now in the hands of the Japanese, was running low. The U.S. government created a film called *Hemp for Victory* to educate farmers on the need for hemp and how to grow it. The government distributed 400,000 pounds of cannabis seeds to farmers, who in turn produced 42,000 tons of hemp fiber each year until 1946.

264. No, You Wouldn't Get High if You Used the Tailpipe as a Bong

Henry Ford's first Model T car was not only made to run on ethanol made from hemp, but also much of the car itself was made from plastic panels made from hemp fibers. Ford claimed that the panels had ten times the impact strength than that of steel panels. He believed that "apples, weeds, sawdust—almost anything" could be made into fuel and sought to explore those options further. Unfortunately, this did not happen because of the easy operation of gasoline engines, the abundance of petroleum from new oil field discoveries, and pressure from the petroleum industry to keep itself the main supplier of fuel. Alternative fuels only became seriously researched more than fifty years later when environmental concerns spurred more attention to the matter.

265. Your Coughing Fits Might Seem Like Death, But You Won't Actually Die

In any given year in America, total deaths from marijuana equal zero. There is no known toxic amount of THC. According to the Merck Index (12th edition), the lethal dose for labs rats was 42 mg/kg of body weight by inhalation or 1270 mg/kg for male rats and 730 mg/kg for females by oral consumption. The actual amount of THC or smoked or consumed marijuana is a highly debated topic, but the general consensus is that it would be virtually impossible for a human to consume enough THC to die from it.

266. Scientists Have Actually Researched Why You Get the Munchies

Have you ever thought, as you ate your third Twinkie, "why am I so hungry when I'm high?" Well, scientists, who are probably all smoking when nobody's looking and coming up with such things as giant flying balloons, also wondered this. Normally, hunger is caused by endocannabinoids—proteins the body synthesizes to create appetite. Research is inconclusive, but so far it points to tetrahydrocannabinol (note the "cannabin" in the name) or THC being accepted by the same protein receptors in your brain that process endocannabinoids. An abundance of this protein equals an abundance of hunger.

267. You Used to Be Able to Pay Taxes with Hemp

That's right. From 1631 until the early nineteenth century, cannabis hemp was accepted as legal tender, to the point taxes could be paid with it. This was mostly done to encourage farms to grow cannabis hemp in lieu of tobacco. Both Thomas Jefferson and George Washington were hemp farmers. Or they owned hemp farms, at least. In any case, if the Puritanical Founding Fathers of our country could agree on one thing, it was the importance of hemp. There was a time when a farmer who did not grow hemp could be jailed.

268. You Know You Want to Smoke 2,700-Year-Old Pot Found in a Chinese Tomb

Almost three millennia ago, an ancient pothead was buried with over two pounds of weed. The scientists who exhumed the stash and its owner in late 2008 reported that the evidence indicates hemp was grown not only for its usefulness in materials, but also for its psychoactive properties (the long-deceased owner had picked the less active male plants out of the pile, leaving the more potent female plants). They further theorized that the weed might have been used in some sort of spiritual ceremony; two pounds of weed is enough to make anyone quite spiritual.

269. If You're Ever in a War, You'll Want This Camouflage Too

In October of 2006, Canadian soldiers in Afghanistan encountered militants who used the ten-foot-tall marijuana forests for cover. When thickly grown, such forests are very good protection against bullets. The soldiers responded by camouflaging their cars in pot plants and trying to burn down the forest to flush militants out of hiding. General Rick Hillier, who oversaw the action, noted of the latter tactic, "A couple of brown plants on the edges of some of those [forests] did catch on fire. But a section of soldiers that was downwind from that had some ill effects and decided that was probably not the right course of action."

270. You Probably Would Tell the Truth with Just the Promise of Cannabis

War on Drugs? How about War *with* Drugs? During World War II, the Office of Strategic Services (OSS) used marijuana to force the truth from captives. As odd as it sounds, the OSS reported that once intoxicated, the captive was "loquacious and free in his impartation of information." How the OSS managed to get the captive to recall anything useful without giggling is as of yet unknown. Perhaps the CIA will leak those documents in the future. Also, maybe during the Iraq War, former President George W. Bush should have used weed as a truth serum instead of waterboarding.

CHAPTER TWELVE

light up, camera, action

The Best Stoner Flicks

"Listen, I know you don't smoke weed . . .
I know this. But I'ma get you high today. 'Cause it's Friday
. . . you ain't got no job . . . and you ain't got shit to do!"

—Smokey, played by Chris Tucker, in *Friday*

271. *Pineapple Express* (2008)

If you combine action-packed, buddy movies with weed, what do you get? *Pineapple Express*. Seth Rogen, as Dale Denton, and James Franco, as Saul Silver, create such memorable scenes as the smoking of the cross joint and the stoned Saul "saving" Dale after he has been arrested. The concept for the movie actually came from producer/cowriter Judd Apatow, who said in an interview with Metromix Chicago, "I was watching *True Romance* back in the late '90s on laserdisc, and I thought, 'Brad Pitt is so funny as this pothead character but there's only one scene. I kind of wish there was a whole movie about that guy.'"

272. *Harold and Kumar Go to White Castle* (2004)

In *Harold and Kumar Go to White Castle*, the two title characters smoke up then set off on a quest to quench their munchies with tasty burgers from White

Castle. If you can't relate to this dire situation, you really need to smoke more. While they might question their future careers and personal choices, Harold (John Cho) and Kumar (Kal Penn) know for certain that reaching White Castle is their immediate goal above all else. Ironically, Penn, a vegetarian, was actually eating soy patties, not the White Castle burgers, when shooting the ultimate triumphant scene.

273. Half Baked (1998)

Before *Chappelle's Show* gave him the long-overdue recognition that you and your weed-worshipping friends always knew he deserved, Dave Chappelle was the star of *Half Baked*. Is there a moment in the movie that doesn't evoke marijuana truth? From weed so good that the characters start floating around to Sir-Smoke-a-Lot's (Chappelle) emotional breakdown while smoking weed, this movie has everything you need. Amazingly, Chappelle later said on *Inside the Actors Studio* that the original script he had written was even funnier than the final product, and that the final script had been turned into "a weed movie for kids."

274. The Big Lebowski (1998)

If you know the Coen brothers' filmography, you know their best movie is neither the Oscar-winning *No Country for Old Men* nor *Fargo*. No, their best movie is *The Big Lebowski*, a bowling spaghetti Western that made Jeff Bridges a legend in the pot community. Any stoner can relate to the Dude (Bridges)—staying in a robe all day, enjoying the carefree life of an unemployed slacker, crashing a car after dropping a lit roach. In fact, before each scene, Bridges often asked the Coen brothers, "Did the Dude burn one on the way over?" If they said he did, Bridges would rub his eyes until they were red.

275. *Friday* (1995)

Friday is a stoner's stoner movie. You can either relate to Craig Jones (Ice Cube), who sits on the porch all day smoking weed, or Smokey (Chris Tucker), who is constantly high and in trouble. The impact of the film is still prominent for the actors today. In an interview with *A.V. Club*, Tucker said, "People come to my house and knock on my door, like little white kids in my neighborhood that I don't even know, and ask me do I want to smoke weed. Hell, no. That movie was 10 years ago."

276. *Apocalypse Now* (1979)

Opinion varies as to whether this is a movie *about* drugs or a movie to go see *when* you're on drugs. Or both. Based loosely on Joseph Conrad's *Heart of Darkness*, this was one of the first major movies to be set during the Vietnam War. A disparate group of soldiers led by Captain Benjamin L. Willard (Martin Sheen) drifts down a dark river, searching for Colonel Walter E. Kurtz (Marlon Brando), who has gone insane and whom they have orders to kill. Along the way, they deal with the incredible violence and horror around them by smoking all of the weed they can get hold of—as well as a few other drugs. During most of the movie shoot, Sam Bottoms, who played Lance B. Johnson, has said he was high on LSD, speed, and weed.

277. Up in Smoke (1978)

If you don't expect a plot in your stoner movie, Cheech and Chong movies are a great experience. The ultimate stoner humor duo from the 1970s made several movies, but *Up in Smoke* is by far the best known. It certainly wasn't famous for the writing. The humor ranges from weird (i.e., best appreciated when high) to gross-out (a joint they smoke is made partly from dog feces). The film ends with Pedro De Pacas (Cheech Marin) and Anthony 'Man' Stoner (Tommy Chong) accidentally winning the Battle of the Bands contest by funneling large amounts of smoke into the audience, who obligingly vote for them. Consequently, the South African Publications Control Board banned the movie because "it might encourage the impressionable youth of South Africa to take up marijuana smoking."

278. Fritz the Cat (1972)

Back in the 1970s, the idea of an animated movie that dealt with drugs, sex, and politics was a lot more daring than it sounds now. However, *Fritz the Cat* kind of made cinematic history by being a political satire that included, among other things, weed. Even after all of these years of depravity and debauchery in cinema, you'll still probably be alarmed with Fritz (Skip Hinnant's voice) smoking four or five joints simultaneously before having passionate sex with Bertha. Or maybe you won't. Despite all of its controversial content, this first-ever X-rated animated movie went on to gross $100 million at the box office.

279. *Easy Rider* (1969)

Do you feel like getting down with 1960s weed culture? Well, *Easy Rider* is the perfect movie to get high to. Midway through the movie, Wyatt (Peter Fonda) and Billy (Dennis Hopper) pick up George (Jack Nicholson) in a small town after they have been arrested. The three decide to head to New Orleans, and that night, while camping, Wyatt and Billy introduce George to smoking weed. George hesitates, but in the end comes around and has a transcendent, almost religious experience as a result of the marijuana. According to Salon.com, the actors actually smoked real weed whenever they were on-screen.

280. *Reefer Madness* (1936)

You have probably heard of this infamous movie because it was rediscovered in the 1970s and became a favorite cult film (especially for anyone who smokes weed). The forgettable cast showed the dangers of using marijuana by dancing wildly (and badly), swearing (or, at any rate, the 1936 cinematic equivalent of swearing), stealing, lying, shooting one another, and going insane. It's hard to believe anyone took this seriously in 1936. The film was almost immediately recut and reissued under a variety of names with an eye to drawing a bigger audience: *Dope Addict, Love Madness,* and *The Burning Question,* among others. In a final indignity to the original makers of the film, it was remade as an off-Broadway musical in 1998 and that musical version was made into a movie in 2005.

Top Movies to Watch High

Nancy Botwin (Mary-Louise Parker): People got stoned for the *Passion of the Christ*? That's disturbing.

Josh Wilson (Justin Chatwin): It's not as disturbing as seeing it not stoned. Religion my ass. It's a straight up snuff film.

—Weeds

281. 1408 (2007)

1408 is one of the creepiest movies to come out in the past ten years. John Cusack plays Mike Enslin, a writer investigating famous haunted hotels who is challenged to stay one night in room 1408 at the Dolphin Hotel in NYC. Rumor has it that no one makes it out alive. What ensues is one freaky occurrence after another; ax-wielding ghosts, bizarre phone calls from the front desk, and uncontrollable suicidal thoughts. Make sure you watch this with someone else while you're stoned. This flick has a high freak-out factor. Also, this movie is adapted from a short story by Stephen King, which means essentially anything King writes can be made into a movie (to watch stoned).

282. Donnie Darko (2001)

Time travel, the apocalypse, and a deranged guy in a bunny suit—it doesn't get much better than that when you're smoking up. Jake Gyllenhaal plays the title character, who is a schizophrenic high-school student who sleepwalks. Once he goes off his meds, he begins to experience some pretty strange things. After finding a book on time travel and talking with his imaginary bunny buddy, things start to fall into place and he realizes the end is near. If the unbelievably creepy music doesn't push you over the edge, then Patrick Swayze as a motivational speaker might. Also, a cool fact: in the party scene, the person wearing a Ronald Reagan mask while jumping on a trampoline is modeled after a photo of pot lover Hunter S. Thompson doing the same thing.

283. Dumb and Dumber (1994)

Lloyd (Jim Carrey) and Harry (Jeff Daniels) are two dim-witted friends who go on a cross-country road trip to return a very important briefcase to Lloyd's dream girl. One of your smartass, stoned friends has probably re-created one of the best scenes, the most annoying sound in the world (according to the DVD feature, "Still Dumb After All These Years," that line and the noise were completely ad-libbed). Watching this movie while stoned takes it to another level. However, you might think it's a good idea to get a bowl haircut or buy a van that looks like a sheepdog.

284. The Goonies (1985)

One of the greatest movies of the '80s is even better while you're stoned. The Walsh brothers (Sean Astin and Josh Brolin), Chunk (Jeff Cohen), Sloth (John

Matuszak), the Fratellis (Joe Pantoliano and Robert Davi), and Data (Jonathan Ke Quan) are twice as hilarious, and the hunt for One-Eyed Willie's buried treasure is even more fun than it was when you were a kid. Also, when you're high and think the pirate ship is real instead of a sound stage, you'll feel vindicated that it was filmed on an actual ship! By the end you'll be jonesing for some Baby Ruths and rocky road ice cream while doing the Truffle Shuffle in your living room.

285. Pee Wee's Big Adventure (1985)

A man-boy with one of the craziest houses ever invented is on a mission to find his stolen bike. The bright colors, hilarious dialogue, and Pee Wee's (Paul Reubens) signature laugh is sure to be even that much funnier while you're wasted. Freak-out alert: When Large Marge picks up Pee Wee in her big rig, you might have an adverse reaction when she is done telling her story. If it can happen when you are a kid, it can happen when you are stoned. Also, the movie might be (very) loosely based on *The Bicycle Thief*. However, even if this is somehow true, a huge difference is you'll become really depressed if you're high and watch *The Bicycle Thief* (in fact, you'll become depressed watching this movie if you're sober).

286. The NeverEnding Story (1984)

Oddly enough, you don't need to be stoned to realize this movie is a trip. Young Bastian (Barret Oliver) might actually have been stoned when he first opened *The NeverEnding Story* in the attic of his school. He is introduced to a Rock Biter, who has a serious case of the munchies for limestone and granite, Falkor the

Luckdragon, and Morla the Aged One, an oversized turtle with an allergy to children. And how about all of those freaky folks at the Ivory Tower? Even though he's only reading the story, he is the only one that can save Fantasia from "the Nothing." Sound strange enough already? If you smoke enough, you might feel like *you* are the one riding on Falkor's back through the lands of Fantasia.

287. 2001: A Space Odyssey (1968)

In April 1968, just after the "Summer of Love," Stanley Kubrick created the perfect movie for all of the pot-smoking hippies who wanted to experience life in outer space. Five scientists aboard a ship headed to Jupiter are terrorized by an artificial intelligence supercomputer named HAL. Everything about this movie screams stoner classic: the music, the special effects, the paranoia that a computer is controlling your life. Also, as an added stoner bonus, the segment of the movie called "Jupiter and Beyond the Infinite" synchs up perfectly with the Pink Floyd song "Echoes" (look it up on YouTube). Just don't forget to come back to Earth when you're done.

288. Help! (1965)

The premise of the movies is simple: the Fab Four try to avoid being killed by a group of religious cult members after Ringo Starr obtains the "sacred sacrificial ring." The Beatles have admitted that the film was shot in a "haze of marijuana," which explains all of the flubbed lines and some of the bizarre scenes and dialogue. In an interview in *The Beatles Anthology*, Ringo said, "A hell of a lot of pot was being smoked while we were making the film. It was great." Their escapades take them to the Bahamas, the Alps, and Buckingham Palace. You'll giggle like a schoolgirl during their wacky antics and know you're having just as much fun as they were.

289. *Alice in Wonderland* (1951)

A pipe-smoking caterpillar, singing flowers, mome raths, and one messed-up tea party: it doesn't get much wackier, unless of course you're flyin' high while watching Disney's take on Lewis Carroll's *Alice in Wonderland*. The eccentric director Tim Burton is revamping this classic tale, which is sure to be even more bizarre than the original. It's due in theaters in 2010, so pack your pipe and take a tumble down the rabbit hole.

290. *The Wizard of Oz* (1939)

Follow the yellow brick road and beware of the flying monkeys. It's really the bright colors and the singing munchkins that make this movie more entertaining while high. Dorothy (Judy Garland), the Scarecrow (Ray Bolger), the Tin Man (Jack Haley), and the Cowardly Lion (Bert Lahr) should have smoked up before starting their journey to the Emerald City. That Wicked Witch (Margaret Hamilton) is one crazy lady and a nice doobie would have taken the edge off. Play Pink Floyd's *Dark Side of the Moon* while you watch it and enjoy an even trippier experience.

CHAPTER THIRTEEN

mixed weedia

The Best Stoner TV Shows

"Okay, let's see, toke as needed. Caution: objects may seem more edible than they actually are."

—Homer Simpson, voiced by Dan Castellaneta, on *The Simpsons*

291. *Weeds*: Ticky-Tacky Baby Bongers

From the highly addictive theme song, which—bombed or not—gets stuck in your head from your first episode, to the compulsively watchable cast of suburban dealers, Showtime's acclaimed series *Weeds* delivers a satisfying buzz. The premise is rather simple (making it easy for stoners to follow): Widow Nancy Botwin (Mary-Louise Parker) starts selling dope to help her family keep up with the Jonses in a fictional Los Angeles burb. Chaos ensues. Costar Kevin Nealon says the show shines a light on pot's prevalence in society. "A lot of baby boomers are baby *bongers*," he said.

292. *That '70s Show*: Enter the Circle

You can catch a contact high watching the crew from *That '70s Show*. Eric (Topher Grace), Donna (Laura Prepon), Michael (Ashton Kutcher), and Jackie (Mila Kunis) toke up in the "Circle," as clever cameramen literally use smoke and mirrors to evoke the psychedelic feeling of being high as a kite in a basement with a shag rug. The premiere episode ruffled feathers when it aired in August 1998 because the teens were drinking beer and smoking (Fox kept the scenes intact but aired an antidrug PSA right after the show). The show was a good launchpad for Kutcher, who went on to star in *Dude, Where's My Car?*, a classic movie to see while stoned.

293. *Rescue Me*: Blazing the Airways

Denis Leary's drug of choice is probably a bottle of rot-gut Irish whiskey, but as the star of FX's popular *Rescue Me*, his character, Tommy Gavin, is forced to deal with his teenage daughter's blazing ways. Oh, yeah, and speaking of Denis and pot, the actor has jokingly claimed Sir Paul McCartney used Heather Mills's artificial leg to smuggle ganja. The actor launched the attack against the Beatles legend and his ex-wife (who lost her leg due to a motorcycle accident in 1993) in his book, *Why We Suck: A Feel-Good Guide to Staying Fat, Loud, Lazy and Stupid*.

294. *Over There*: FX Does It Again

With a character named Maurice "Smoke" Williams (Sticky Fingaz), you know someone's getting high. Add FX to the mix and it's all but a given. In Stephen Bocco's gritty, short-lived Iraqi war drama, *Over There*, soldiers toke up. In an article in *USA Today*, co-creator and executive producer Chris Gerolmo said, "the show's depiction of pot use is not an endorsement." However, he later says, "drug use is certainly part of life in the Army." Streetwise "Smoke" lit up in the premiere episode, and his backstory has him high for most of his twenty years growing up in Compton (naturally, home of the Chronic).

295. *Entourage*: East Coast, West Coast Connex

Ari Gold (Jeremy Piven): "Smoke more weed, Turtle. Seriously, smoke more weed." You can learn a lot from Vince (Adrian Grenier) and his entourage, NYC transplants who quickly learn that a weed hookup opens doors in Hollywood. While they *all* light up, Turtle (Jerry Ferrara) is the resident pothead. Off the show, Ferrara has quit the bud, so what's really in Turtle's bong? "I just smoke regular [American Spirit] tobacco. . . . It looks like weed smoke, but it's really harsh the tenth take. Everyone thinks it's real. . . . [I]f I smoked that much weed while working, it would be the worst show in the world. Or at least my character would be the worst character in the world."

296. *Family Guy*: The Pot Musical

Family Guy is normally a great show to watch high, but episode 12, "420," in season seven is stoner brilliance. Brian (creator Seth MacFarlane's voice) gets thrown in the slammer for drug possession, then launches a musical campaign to legalize weed. Mayor West (Adam West's voice) passes the law, and the whole town goes to pot. Sadly, MacFarlane has since sworn off Mary Jane. He says, "I don't smoke much pot anymore. One of the last times I was stoned, I was convinced that I would die unless I kept moving my body. So I sat there, baked, waving my arms around like a crazy person." Dude, what's wrong with crazy?

297. Brain on Drugs? Flip to Noggin!

You've probably already got your DVR set to record these kids shows so that when you're good and blitzed, you can break out the Cool Ranch Doritos and Oreos and sink into the couch for a fun trip. But just in case, here are the Top Kids Shows to Watch

When High: *Yo Gabba Gabba!* (psychedelically attired DJ Lance spins for his gang of colorful characters who dance and sing); *Teletubbies* (colorful puppet-people dance and sing, freaky for sure); *Boohbah* (colorful puppets spin, bounce, and fly); *The Wiggles* (what do those Aussies put in their fruit salad to make it so "yummy"?); *Sesame Street* (ever wonder why Cookie Monster has such a *serious* case of the munchies?); and *SpongeBob SquarePants* (if you like Bob, you'll *love* SpongeBong HempPants).

298. Bob Ross, Happy Little High

Jury's out on whether Bob Ross from PBS's *Joy of Painting* smoked up—or was just high on life. Today, his pure aura has given way to a cult following. But you know the minute he put paint to canvas, bongs across the nation came out of hiding in honor of happy little trees everywhere. If the fast-food industry knew what they owed this afro'ed artiste, they'd color the French fries box in crimson, ochre, and sky blue. Ross described the popularity of his painting technique: "We're like drug dealers, come into town and get everybody absolutely addicted to painting. It doesn't take much to get you addicted."

299. Anything on Adult Swim

If it's late at night and you've just smoked a bowl, Cartoon Network's Adult Swim is the perfect place to land. The old-school shows like *Space Ghost Coast to Coast*, *Sealab 2021*, *The Brak Show* were absurdly classic in their amusing adaptations of old Hanna-Barbera cartoons. The present shows like *Aqua Teen Hunger Force*, *Tim and Eric Awesome Show*, *The Mighty Boosh*, and *Robot Chicken* have taken on a whole new humorous dimension of insanity. Also, how could you argue with that *ATHF* episode where Shake needs weed for his glaucoma, and the Mooninites come down to offer him some "Moonajuana"?

300. *Flight of the Conchords:* High as a Kite Flying from New Zealand to New York

If you live in Toronto, you might find a Craigslist posting under Casual Encounters that reads, "Want to smoke weed and watch *Flight of the Conchords*?" Dude, lucky you if you live in Toronto, eh? If you've ever watched the show, you'll notice that the guys, a native New Zealand folk-rock comedy duo named Bret (Bret McKenzie) and Jemaine (Jemaine Clement) *appear* to be supersober, but their stoner ways are waaaay too strong for this to actually be the case. In the opening scene from HBO's cult favorite, the guys are even shown flying over an animated cityscape of NYC. Their wackadoo songs will cause you to have tears of stoned laughter.

The Sound of Stoners

"So what if I'm smokin' weed onstage and doing what I gotta do? It's not me shooting nobody, stabbing nobody, killing nobody. It's a peaceful gesture and they have to respect that and appreciate that."

—Snoop Dogg, rapper

301. Pink Floyd

Before you do anything else, light a candle, take a hit off of that joint, and play *The Dark Side of the Moon* by Pink Floyd. You're in for a one-of-a-kind experience. This album was created to be listened to while on some form of hallucinogenic, but if you want a really mellow experience, pot will be just fine. It's one of the greatest albums in the world for a reason. Next move on to *The Wall* to inspire the rebellious teenager in you to break free from conformity. Pink Floyd knew how to create an album so it told a story. It's a journey, so light up and enjoy.

302. Phish

Since the 1980s, Phish has been appealing to the new generation of hippies or hippie wannabes. You can only truly appreciate Phish when you're stoned. You can keep up with those twenty-minute-long songs and concerts that sometimes go all night (at Phish's 2000 New Year's Party in the Everglades, the band played for almost eight hours). You also need to completely zone out and jam out to Trey Anastasio's nasty solos. Fans of Phish, or the aptly named Phishheads, are very loyal to the band and even follow them around the world.

303. The Grateful Dead

If you're feeling nostalgic, it's time to toke up with one of the most famous weed-loving bands, the Grateful Dead. The original kings of psychedelic stoner rock are legends and offer some of the best jams to smoke to. Songs like "Casey Jones," "Uncle John's Band," and "Sugar Magnolia" are some of the classics. Jerry Garcia, one of the founding members of the band, has become like a God in the eyes of Deadheads. Sadly, Garcia passed in August 1995 from a heart attack. Also, be sure to grab a pint of Ben & Jerry's Cherry Garcia to satisfy the munchies.

304. Dave Matthews Band

You might not immediately associate this band with pot, but go to any of their shows and you'll be greeted with a cloud of smoke. The quintessential college band, Dave Matthews Band has a legion of followers who tour the country in their dad's Volvo to catch the shows. DMB's music isn't like the typical stoner tunes of Phish or the Dead, but it will do the trick. The band's fans are usually the type of folks you would see playing Frisbee on the quad wearing Tevas and eating Kashi, but as soon as graduation arrives they'll turn into investment bankers. How Dave's music breeds pot smokers no one is sure, but they are an undeniable combination.

305. The Beatles

The Beatles started to experiment heavily with drugs in the mid-1960s, after the "I Wanna Hold Your Hand" days, but before "Sgt. Pepper." Just listening to the progression of the albums, you can clearly see how drugs influenced their writing process. This is most clear during "Lucy in the Sky with Diamonds," "Strawberry Fields Forever," and the incredibly creepy eight-minute track "Revolution 9," found on *The White Album*. Also, when you think about it when high, that whole "I am the walrus" will blow your mind.

306. Bob Marley

Ya mon! You can't think of Bob Marley without thinking about weed. They're like peanut butter and jelly: a perfect combination. A Jamaican-born singer and song-writer, Bob Marley still is the epitome of reggae and the Rastafarian belief system. As a Rasta, he believed in smoking ganja as a spiritual act. Rastafarians believe it is a sacrament that cleanses the mind, body, and soul and brings them closer to God. At the age of thirty-six, he developed melanoma that quickly metastasized and he died in 1981. Smoke this one for Bob.

307. Cypress Hill

Are you feeling "insane in the membrane"? You are if you're listening to Cypress Hill while smoking a fat joint. A hip-hop group from Los Angeles, Cypress Hill quickly rose to the top of the charts in the early '90s. With their songs, like "I Wanna Get High," "Stoned Is the Way of the Walk," and "Hits from the Bong," Cypress Hill became outspoken advocates for the legalization of marijuana. They were even banned from *Saturday Night Live* after one of the members smoked can-nabis on-air and the band trashed their instruments.

308. Snoop Dogg

No rapper has been more synonymously associated with pot than Snoop D-O-double G. From his start in the early '90s, he's always talked about smoking weed in his songs and has gotten in his share of trouble for being in possession. After many legal troubles, he announced in 2002 that he was giving up marijuana for good, but it didn't take. So, throw on some "Gin and Juice," smoke a blunt, and do Snoop proud—fo shizzle.

309. Bob Dylan

Just the mention of Bob Dylan should make you want to light up. In the time of beatniks, Dylan played the local coffeehouses in Greenwich Village, protested the war in Vietnam, and built a following of peace-loving, like-minded fans. Smoking pot was becoming more popular and some credit Dylan for turning them onto it. It's even been said that Dylan was the one who introduced the Beatles to weed. He is the voice of the counterculture and is still going strong today.

310. The Doors

C'mon baby, light my joint. Like most bands of the '60s, the Doors smoked a lot of weed. Their music represented both the calm and soothing effects of smoking and the angry, rebellious times of that era. Jim Morrison's hypnotic voice is sure to take you to another place while you're stoned. Try "Riders on the Storm," "The End," and "Light My Fire," to start. The Doors got into a heap of trouble while on *The Ed Sullivan Show*, when they refused to change one of the lyrics to remove a drug reference and Morrison sang "Girl we couldn't get much higher." Needless to say, Eddie was not happy and banned them from the show.

Smoking and Gaming

"We all used to smoke weed all day instead of working, and we'd just play video games for months on end. But we all really wanted to work and make movies."

—Seth Rogen, actor

311. The Halo Series (Xbox)

Halo is the legendary console first-person shooter known for bringing frat boys and gaming nerds together to kill aliens. Much has been made of its coop versus multiplayer modes, but less has been said about its role as a stress relief toy. Try this: the next time you get ripped and play a Halo game with friends, do not fire your weapons. Just run around clubbing the shit out of people until everyone quits. You will die constantly, but there will be moments when you will completely ruin things for other people with a swift knock on the skull. Gives "buzz kill" a whole new meaning.

312. Gun Fight (Arcade)

Gun Fight came out in 1975. Before you assume it required you to type things in like "Go North" or "Examine Corpse," you should know that Gun Fight was the Halo of its day. For one quarter at the arcade, you and a friend receive a limited amount of time to shoot each other on as many maps (and there are several) as you can. This game has it all: cacti, ultraviolence, chuckwagons—who needs pistol whipping and crazy alien swords? And if you have no friends, never fear: just smoke up and shoot the chuckwagon. It's only a quarter, and in this case, that's the same value as it was in 1975.

313. Super Mario Kart (SNES)

Mario isn't jumping down any pipes in this game, so be sure to pack an extra one for him. Battle mode is king here: when you sicken of racing your friends (that one guy just won't lose), you can get revenge by throwing shells at them. The later games are more technically brilliant, but the early Kart game lacks the frustratingly unfair rubber-band. Also, almost everyone has played it at least once, which avoids too many "how do I turn around" and "what's the banana do" complications from the less-videogame oriented of your friends.

314. Super Mario Bros. 2 (NES)

Redheaded franchise stepchild Super Mario Bros. 2 features all of the following: potions that explode into doors, a mouse that throws high-powered explosives, a cross-dressing dinosaur who uses the very eggs he incubates as weapons, a floating princess, a giant frog named after a skin condition, a mask that chases you when you steal its key from within the jar it inhabits, a nightmare bizarro world filled with money, floating cherries, and that weird running thing Luigi does when he jumps. All of these things will feel much more ordinary after a few bong hits.

315. Rock Band 1 and 2 (Multiple Consoles)

Two-thirds sex, drugs, and rock 'n' roll, the Rock Band games were seemingly made for stoners. For one, they involve music. If you haven't wanted to play music while high, you are not human. Second, the music is easy to play. Alright, it's just colored buttons and it will never translate into real-world talent until someone invents the coloritar. You can get in on inventing that. Also, you should try to remember to use your star power ("Overdrive"), just in case you screw up playing your instrument of choice while you're high.

316. Animal Crossing (Various Nintendo Consoles)

Killing people all the time can really kill your buzz. Take a break and go fishing. Talk with animal friends who display an alarming tendency to ignore your advice. Buy some furniture. Plant some trees. You can do what you like; it's sort of like Grand Theft Auto, except instead of blowing up police cars, you can mail a toy to your mom. Animal Crossing allows you to do all the things you sometimes think you should do, only you get to do them from the comfort of your own couch. And with talking animals.

317. Katamari Damacy (PlayStation 2)

The people who designed Katamari Damacy *must* have been high—get this: while on a bender, the King of All Cosmos has scattered the constellations from the sky. Since he has better things to do (such as nursing his hangover while puking up rainbows and finding new codpieces), he has sent you, the Prince, to make new stars by rolling up objects from Earth. Katamari Damacy is great if you go with a gravity theme for the night; make yourself a gravity bong and go to town making stars out of candies and little Japanese people. In case you were wondering, none of the above has been embellished.

318. Planescape: Torment (PC)

While most of the games on the list are great for playing with groups of friends or audiences, Planescape: Torment is more of an individual experience. The least combat intensive but most philosophical of the Infinity Engine games (see also: Baldur's Gate II), the game opens with you on a slab in the morgue trying to piece together your inability to die. The world in which you live is one where anything can warp you to a different planet or dimension: you might pick up a rock and find yourself in an ocean, or walk through a door only to fall from a cliff. Also, your best friend is a floating skull (though there is never an option to poke a hole in him and use him as a bong).

319. Madden: Whatever Year It Is (Multiple Consoles)

The Madden football games have always been great, from their early days where players were differentiated only by the numbers on their backs, to the modern-day "hey, I can zoom in and see pores" sequels. The home version allows you to join in on the fun without fear of a urine test to disqualify you. Even if you hate sports, there's something to love about the Madden series, and if you start losing consistently, just call special teams plays to confuse the shit out of people. If football isn't your thing, the NHL hockey series is the frozen north equivalent dynasty game of choice.

320. Seaman (Dreamcast)

Not a game so much as an experience, Seaman was one of the weirder entries to the virtual pet genre. Seaman is a fish with a human face. You talk to him via the microphone on your Dreamcast controller. He'll ask you questions, and sometimes he'll go off on a particular topic. Part of the fun to Seaman is freaking out your roommates by talking into a controller for twenty minutes. The other is watching him eat his brothers in his pupal stage. You don't need to be high to feel Seaman's enlightenment, but it certainly helps.

A Stash of Standup

"High Times magazine is a notch intellectually below Highlights for Children. I mean, they're both great to read when you're baked, but come on, ya know . . ."

—David Cross, standup comedian

321. Bill Hicks: Pot Advocate

You gotta love Bill Hicks. "Marijuana should be legal. Shut up and smoke that. It's the law." But when you pair this full-on pro-pot comic with Reagan-era brain-on-drugs BS, you're just asking for an enlightened trip. Hicks passed away before he could experience legalized weed, but he envisioned it in a purple haze. "That would be a nice world, wouldn't it? Quiet, mellow, hungry, high people everywhere. Domino's pizza trucks everywhere." He's probably up there smoking with Jimi Hendrix and Elvis right now.

322. Doug Benson: Pot PSA Backfires

Star of *Super High Me*, Doug Benson, the almost *Last Comic Standing*, is riding the ganja gravy train to the biggest stash of good shit he can get his hands on, as he riffs on an antidrug PSA: "So the girl is melting into the couch . . . I'm watching that commercial going, how do I get a hold of some of that weed? That is some amazing shit that I would like to try. I've been smoking the Can't-Find-My-Keys weed, and somewhere in the world there is some Melting-Into-the-Couch shit. That would be an incredible ride. Plus, if I melted into the couch, maybe I'd find my keys."

323. Sarah Silverman: Everything's Better with Weed

Now, what's a nice Jewish girl from New Hampshire doing getting high in movies . . . on the boob tube . . . and backstage? She's vaporized with fellow comic Doug Benson in *Super High Me*, taken a biiiiiig bong hit (then kissed herself in the mirror) at the end of *Jesus Is Magic*, and toked up to calm the fuck down before hitting the stage in Hollywood recently for a standup act in which her material revolved around her tabloid breakup from Jimmy Kimmel. You can't blame Sarah. When you're feeling freaked, a toke will mellow you somethin' nice.

324. Katt Williams: It's Just a Plant

He may be a pimp, but Katt Williams has a point about pot. "It's just a plant. It just grow like that. And if you happen to set it on fire, there are some effects. But that's not the same as drugs. So why the fuck is [it] illegal? Aspirin is perfectly legal, but if you take 13 of them, that'll be your last headache. Long as you be living you ain't never heard of a motherfuckin' overdose on marijuana. . . . *He ain't dead*. He gonna wake up in 30 minutes, hungry enough to eat up everything in your house. That's the side effects: hungry, happy, sleepy. That's it!"

325. Tommy Davidson: Sending Scooby Up in Smoke

Here's a comic that poses the existential question for all of you kids of the '70s: what would Scooby Doo do? Well, naturally, he'd roll a fatty and then join Shaggy in the van to light up. "Scooby smoke weed. I mean, come on, he rode around in a van with the flowers on the side, on a Saturday morning, looking for a haunted house. Tell me they wasn't high. He hung around with Shaggy! He never shaved, he wore the same bell bottoms every damn day. . . . They *always* had the munchies. . . . 'Scoob is that a sandwich?' Like if you find a sandwich in a haunted house you'd eat that shit."

326. Eddie Izzard: Founder of the Stoned Olympics

Performance-enhancing drugs are banned at the Olympics, but standup comedian and "Lost Python" Eddie Izzard advocates for performance-*debilitating* drugs. "Smoke a joint and win the 100 meters. . . . [W]e should have a Stoned Olympics!" Athletes are tested for drugs to make sure they've taken enough; a ceremonial joint is lit in Athens; opening ceremonies feature brightly painted children who nosh on hash brownies. "[This is] not like the normal Olympics where you get up at 6 in the morning and train hard and run a race, but you get up at 2 in the afternoon, get down to the track where you're handed a slice of pizza and you're off!" Favorite event? The high jump.

327. George Carlin: Old-School Stoner

Revered in cannabis circles and beyond as a standup legend, George Carlin talked pot in a *Playboy* interview that dates back to 1982. Can you dig it? "I was a stonehead for 30 years. I'd wake up in the morning and if I couldn't decide whether I wanted to smoke a joint or not, I'd smoke a joint to figure it out. And I stayed high all day long. When people asked me, 'Do you get high to go onstage?' I could never understand the question. I mean, I'd been high since eight that morning. Going onstage had nothing to do with it."

328. Dave Chappelle: New-School Stoner

The smoke-filled comedic genius of Dave Chappelle is undeniable. If you haven't heard of this hilarious, straight-talking, pot-smoking funnyman, well, it might be time to put down the pipe and pay attention for a few minutes. In his comedy routine, "Weed plus Gay Shit," Chappelle explains why he enjoys smoking weed with white people: "All white people talk about when they get high is other times they got high. I could listen to that shit all night. 'Dude, remember at Frank's last week—I was fucking smashed!'"

329. Nick Swardson: Dr. Dre Protegé

The dude who took a line from Dr. Dre and turned it into a household name for stoners, Nick Swardson is the guy who *smokes weed every day*. That is, until he quit. "I totally smoked for a while and then I totally stopped and my friends were all like, '. . . What? . . . You quit? . . . You're done? Really? That sucks. . . . What are you doing? That sucks. . . .' I'm like yeah, it *really* sucks remembering where I put stuff now. The whole first week I thought I was psychic. I thought I had new powers all of a sudden. . . . I'd be like where are my keys? Oh, they're in my pocket. *How did I know that?"*

330. Arj Barker: High on Life

Comedian Arj Barker, co-creator of the *Marijuana-Logues*, saw a flyer for a place you'd only want to visit if you were very, *very* high. "It forced me to ask a burning question: Would my body be able to physically survive the amount of dope I would need to smoke in order to visit a *Shoeseum*? I didn't *always* smoke pot. In fact for years and years, Arj Barker was high . . . on . . . *life*! But eventually, I built up a tolerance. I used to seize the day, but pretty soon I was seizing one day, two days, three days, four days, up to a week just to cop the same buzz."

CHAPTER FOURTEEN

celebrities and politicians who got higher in life

Celebrities Who Toke Up

"The reason we're so dangerous is because we're totally harmless."

—Cheech Marin, actor

331. Woody Harrelson: His *Natural Born Killers* Character Really Should Have Mellowed Out

Woody Harrelson, who you might remember played the innocent and loveable Woody Boyd in *Cheers*, is a huge supporter and activist for the legalization of marijuana and hemp. With fame comes attention, and he's seen his fair share of trouble concerning his views on pot. On June 1, 1996, he was arrested in Kentucky after he planted four hemp seeds. He did this to challenge the state law that did not distinguish between industrial hemp and marijuana. Harrelson actually won the case and it was a big victory for the weed-smoking community.

332. Matthew McConaughey: Starring in *Dazed and Confused* Was Only the Beginning

Picture this: An A-list actor found screaming like a banshee, playing the bongos and completely naked. Just another day in the life of Matthew McConaughey. On October 26, 1999, he was arrested at his home after someone called the police reporting a disturbance. He was also in possession of marijuana. He denied the drug charges and was only charged with disturbing the peace. You've probably done some crazy things while high, but McConaughey has to be the first to play the bongos, naked, and loud enough for the cops to be called.

333. Kristen Stewart: If You Smoke Weed and Are a Vampire, You Have a Shot with Her

Kristen Stewart, who played Bella Swan in *Twilight*, isn't as innocent as the character she played. On November 26, 2008, the same month that *Twilight* rose to the top of the box office, Kristen was seen taking a hit off of a pipe while sitting on the steps of her house. By the way she was dressed, Stewart looked like she was in a wake-and-bake situation. She's also been photographed wearing a pot leaf bikini. Can you really blame her though? Being a vampire's girlfriend can't be all it's cracked up to be.

334. Jack Black: The Embodiment of Cannabis Classiness

As a past recipient of smoker of the year by *High Times* magazine, Jack Black seems to have dedicated his entire career to cannabis. You can get stoned and laugh to the acoustic, heavy metal, comedy of his band Tenacious D. You can also watch him in movie roles where he's either on drugs (*Tropic Thunder*, *Orange County*) or help enhance your own high (*Be Kind Rewind*, *The School of Rock*). However, when asked about how often he smokes nowadays in a 2009 interview with Maxim.com, Jack Black said, "It's basically limited to celebratory Js on special occasions. I did smoke the other day before a meeting, and it was a big mistake. I'm a lightweight, and if I smoke really powerful weed, I get paranoid and nonverbal."

335. Charlize Theron: She Could Definitely Pull Off Playing a Stoner

This Academy Award–winning actress is not only drop-dead gorgeous, but also loves to smoke up. She was photographed smoking out of a homemade apple bong in her backyard and then having a giggling fit. The star of *Monster*, *North Country*, and *The Italian Job* hasn't commented publicly on her love of smoking, but, who knows, she might still smoke with you. Sometimes anything seems possible when you're high. Also, in season three of *Arrested Development*, her guest appearances as Rita might seem like she's stoned, but she's really not (Mr. F!).

336. Cameron Diaz: She's Not Really Ditsy, She Just Smokes a Lot of Weed

She's a life-long pot smoker and one of the most successful actresses out there right now. This blond bombshell has openly discussed her love of weed and loves to smoke with friends. Cameron has been photographed smoking up with ex-boyfriend Justin Timberlake and *Charlie's Angels* costar and gal pal Drew Barrymore. Have you ever wondered about all of the constant giggling and silly dance moves in that movie? Well, that explains it.

337. Seth Rogen: Are Pot Movies Allowed to Be Made If He *Isn't* the Star?

The star of *Knocked Up*, *Superbad*, and *Pineapple Express* has brought smoking pot back into mainstream culture again. These flicks are not only hilarious, but also celebrate marijuana like no one has since Cheech and Chong. In an interview by Jon Stewart on *The Daily Show*, Rogen encouraged kids to drop out of school, smoke a lot of weed, and write a movie about it. If it worked for him, it can work for you.

338. Whitney Houston and Bobby Brown: Crack Is Whack, But Dope Is . . . Dope

If it wasn't obvious to you that Whitney and Bobby like to smoke up, you soon found out in their short-lived Bravo series *Being Bobby Brown*. That kind of crazy behavior can only be caused by one thing—and they weren't high on life. It's been said for years that Bobby was the downfall of Whitney's career and the reason she started using drugs in the first place. This may or may not be true, but they sure looked like they were having a fun time on that show. In 2000, Houston got in trouble for bringing 15.2 grams of weed on a plane. Shortly after *Being Bobby Brown* ended, Bobby and Whitney divorced.

339. Carrie Fisher: Maybe Her Dealer Was Yoda

Of course Princess Leia tokes up! She openly admitted to smoking between takes of *Star Wars* and dabbling in harder drugs on the weekends. She has said, "I always wanted to blunt and blur what was painful. My idea [in taking drugs] was pain reduction and mind expansion, but I ended up with mind reduction and pain expansion." Can you imagine Leia and Chewbacca smoking up?

340. Barbra Streisand: Rollin' with Brolin?

Who knew that Yentl liked to get high? Babs did an interview for *Rolling Stone* in 1972 in which she admitted to smoking joints onstage. She said, "I'd take out a joint and light it. First, just faking it. Then I started lighting live joints, passing them around to the band, you know. It was great; it relieved all my tensions. And I ended up with the greatest supply of grass ever." She might not have become a toker for life, but like any good citizen of the '70s, she did her fair share.

Stoners in the News

"[Quentin Tarantino and I] talked about [Inglourious Basterds], talked about back story, talked about movies to the wee hours of the night. And I got up the next morning, I saw five empty bottles of wine laying on the floor—five—and something that resembled a smoking apparatus—I don't know what that was about—and apparently I had agreed to do the movie because six weeks later, I was in uniform and I was Lieutenant Aldo Raine."

—Brad Pitt, actor

341. The Bong Olympics

Michael Phelps became the Olympic golden child in the summer of 2008 when he won a record-breaking eight gold medals in swimming. Then he was busted for smoking a bong. Many called for his disqualification from the 2012 Olympic Games in London, but Phelps did some damage control, saying, "I engaged in behavior which was regrettable and demonstrated bad judgment." The U.S. Anti-Doping Agency apparently accepted Phelps' apology, but it seems like the only "hit" he'll be taking now is one to his wallet due to the ad campaigns that dropped him after the "incident." If you think about it, he deserves additional medals if he was high while swimming.

342. M-E-T-H-O-D *Man!*

You may know him as a member of the Wu-Tang Clan and as half of the rap duo Method Man and Redman, but that doesn't mean he's above the law. In 2007, Method Man was pulled over by one of New York's finest near NYC's Battery Tunnel. When he rolled down his window, the smell of marijuana was unmistakable. A source quoted in the *New York Daily News* described the scene as being "like something out of Cheech and Chong." The officer also saw blunts and marijuana sitting on the passenger seat. Method Man was arrested but managed to avoid jail time by agreeing to do public service announcements warning about the "dangers" of smoking pot.

343. What a Jackass

You have probably seen former *Jackass* stuntman Steve-O's mug shots flashed on MTV over the past few years. Steve-O (real name Steven Glover) made the news in 2003 when he was arrested for smuggling pot into Sweden during his "Don't Try This at Home" tour. According to HighTimes.com, he swallowed a condom filled with pot and was basically waiting for it to make an appearance so he could smoke it. He ended up paying a $6,700 fine and was good to go. Steve-O checked himself into rehab in 2008. You'll have to wait and see if it takes.

344. "I Am the Walrus" Even Starts to Make Sense

You're probably not surprised to see the Beatles included in this chapter. Individually, the band members all made news with their marijuana use. This includes George Harrison, who, along with his bride-to-be, was arrested for marijuana possession on his wedding day in 1969, and John Lennon, who was almost deported from the United States for marijuana possession. Collectively the band made news in the summer of 1967 when, according to Barry Miles's *Paul McCartney*, they bought a full-page ad in the *Times* titled "The law against marijuana is immoral in principle and unworkable in practice." Marijuana laws in the UK haven't changed too much, but at least they tried, right?

345. Migraine Mishaps

You know Kareem Abdul-Jabbar (born Lew Alcindor) as a highly successful basketball player. But did you know that he's also a pothead? According to Abdul-Jabbar's autobiography *Giant Steps*, he first tried pot at the age of seventeen. He called it "one of his first major individual decisions." Abdul-Jabbar paid a fine for possession of marijuana in 1998 and was arrested in 2000 for driving under the influence of marijuana. He blamed his marijuana use on the nausea that goes along with his painful migraine headaches. Pot is used to relieve nausea—too bad the cops don't see it that way.

346. Hit One Out of the Park

Who is Orlando Cepeda, you ask? Well, he played baseball for the San Francisco Giants, St. Louis Cardinals, and the Boston Red Sox, among others. That's not why he's important here though. In 1966, he unsuccessfully tried to smuggle 160—yes 1-6-0—pounds of marijuana from Puerto Rico to Miami. In 1978, he was sentenced to ten years in prison on drug possession charges and was arrested again in 2007 when police found marijuana, syringes, and coke in his car. Guess old habits die hard! It doesn't seem to have hurt his career though; he was inducted into the Baseball Hall of Fame in Cooperstown, New York, in 1999.

347. Turn On, Tune In, Drop Out

The philosopher/author/proponent of psychedelic drug research Timothy Leary was arrested in 1965 for marijuana possession. Leary's daughter was the one caught with the drugs while returning to the United States from Mexico, but Leary took responsibility. Bet you wish your family would be so generous! Under the Marihuana Tax Act, Leary was sentenced to thirty years in prison, ordered to pay $30,000 in fines, and required to undergo psychiatric tests (many of which he had designed and put into practice). The conviction was overturned in 1969, but Leary was sent back to jail for a 1968 offense. He escaped from prison and fled to Europe. He was recaptured in Afghanistan in 1973 and given a sentence of ninety-five years but was later released in 1976.

348. If Only That Rehab Song Was Stuck in the Singer's Head Too

Britain's—and your—favorite smoker is songstress Amy Winehouse. You probably kind of doubt that it's just pot she's smoking, but she was arrested in 2007 with her husband at the time, Blake Fielder-Civil, in Norway for marijuana possession. According to Us Magazine.com, the couple was released after paying a $715 fine. In 2008, according to the *Sun* newspaper, Winehouse was admitted to the hospital, not because of an adverse reaction to antidrug medication as her representatives claimed, but for excessive marijuana use. Winehouse has actually been in and out of rehab multiple times over the past couple of years, but at this point maybe she should actually stick it out!

349. Get Out of the Way!

In 2002, then-Oakland Raiders receiver Randy Moss was found to be in possession of marijuana during a traffic stop. You might think, marijuana possession, whatever. However, knocking the arresting officer over with his car during said traffic stop, is a bad idea. Moss pled guilty to both offenses and was ordered to pay a $1,200 fine and perform forty hours of community service. This wasn't the first or the last time Moss would be in trouble for marijuana possession, however. According to NBCSports.com, Moss lost his college scholarship at Florida State because of his marijuana use. And, in 2005, Moss admitted his pot use on national TV during an interview with Bryant Gumbel.

350. Medicinal Marijuana on *The Montel Show*

Talk show host Montel Williams was diagnosed with multiple sclerosis (MS) in 1999 and suffered severe, debilitating leg pain caused by nerve damage. Nothing seemed to help. After contemplating suicide, Williams tried pot to see if it could take away his symptoms. In a letter to Connecticut governor Jodi Rell, Williams wrote, "Three puffs and within minutes the excruciating pain in my legs subsided. I had my first restful sleep in months." Turns out that some people didn't care about Williams' pain relief. He was detained at a Detroit airport in 2004 when security found a pipe with marijuana residue in his luggage. According to the Associated Press, Williams paid the $100 fine and went on his way.

Pot and Politicians

"Forty million Americans smoked marijuana; the only ones who didn't like it were Judge Ginsberg, Clarence Thomas and Bill Clinton."

—Jay Leno, host of *The Jay Leno Show*

351. "I Did Not Inhale!"

Perhaps you think of Bill Clinton as one of the first "cool" U.S. presidents. He played saxophone, got lucky with the White House intern, and actually admitted having some type of experience with pot. In 1992, Clinton admitted his marijuana experimentation in an article published by the *New York Times*: "When I was in England, I experimented with marijuana a time or two, and I didn't like it, and I didn't inhale, and I never tried it again." However, despite Clinton's admission, the largest number of marijuana arrests in American history were made during the Clinton administration: over 4,175,357 Americans were arrested on marijuana charges between 1992 and 1999.

352. Al Gore Is Such a Follower

Hey, if President Clinton can admit to smoking pot, why wouldn't Vice President Al Gore want to jump on that bandwagon? Actually, Gore admitted his marijuana use in 1987 when he was basically outed by John Warnecke, Gore's former friend and colleague. If you have a friend who's a narc like Warnecke, put down this book and drop him from your speed dial. Keeping in touch just isn't worth it. Obviously, this breaking news didn't affect Gore too much. He's now an environmental activist, and God knows you don't care if he smoked a fat one.

353. Senator Equals Smuggler

Who is Ralph David Abernathy? you may be asking. Abernathy was a Democratic Georgia senator when he was caught at the Hartsfield International Airport in Atlanta for trying to smuggle seven grams of marijuana into the United States from Jamaica (of course). Where was the pot you may be asking? Surely he didn't just stick it in his carry-on bag? Nope! Abernathy tried to smuggle the pot in his underwear! He was caught when a drug-sniffing dog caught a whiff. According to the *Atlanta Journal-Constitution*, Abernathy wasn't arrested but only had to pay a $500 civil fine.

354. A Royal Debacle

You'd think it would take more than reefer to send the royal family into a tizzy after all they've been through over the past few years, but that wasn't the case in 2002 when Prince Harry admitted to smoking "cannabis." CNN.com reported that "Harry, third in line to the British throne, confessed to his father that he smoked marijuana and drank heavily at a pub . . . last summer, when he was 16." Prince Charles basically flipped out, mainly because marijuana possession is punishable by up to five years in prison. However, Prince Harry was instead forced to attend a one-day rehab program where he was taught "all about the dangers of substance abuse."

355. Newt Fesses Up

The main surprise about Newt Gingrich's admission of smoking marijuana is the fact that he has been a tireless opponent of marijuana legalization and decriminalization for years. In 1982, Gingrich wrote a letter supporting medicinal marijuana that appeared in the *Journal of the American Medical Association*. In 1996, Gingrich told the *Wall Street Journal* that "smoking marijuana was a sign we were alive and in graduate school in that era." Apparently that warm and fuzzy feeling didn't stay with him for long. Later that year, Gingrich introduced a bill that proposed a mandatory death penalty sentence for anyone caught smuggling fifty plus grams of marijuana into the United States. Wow! Thankfully, the proposal did not pass.

356. No Wonder He Couldn't Spell Potato

When you hear the name Dan Quayle, *intelligence* may not be the first word that pops into your mind. According to the *New York Times*, right before the presidential election in 1988, accused drug dealer and convicted bomber Brett Kimberlin set up a press conference to out Quayle's drug use. The press conference was quickly canceled, and Kimberlin was put in solitary confinement. Kimberlin told WBAI radio in New York, "[Quayle] found out that I had marijuana available at the time . . . and he asked if I had any for sale. . . . I thought it was kind of strange. He looked kind of straight. I thought he might be a narc at first."

357. Don't Say It If You Don't Want Everyone to Know . . .

Michael Bloomberg was a candidate for New York City mayor in 2001 when he was asked if he had ever tried pot. You'll find his answer was refreshing! Bloomberg responded, "You bet I did. And I enjoyed it!" An honest answer, but one Bloomberg came to regret after he became mayor and the National Organization for the Reform of Marijuana Laws (NORML) latched onto his words and made them into a full-fledged campaign to convince Bloomberg to legalize and decriminalize marijuana. In a $50,000 campaign, NORML has broadcasted Bloomberg's enthusiastic words on city buses, telephone booths, and even in a *New York Times* advertisement. Thanks for being honest, Mayor!

358. If He Wouldn't Tell the Truth about Iraq, Why Would He Be Honest about His Pot Use?

When George W. Bush admitted that he had a drinking problem in his youth, you'd think he would have just come clean about any other drug problems as well. Surprise, surprise! That didn't happen. Instead, according to BBC News.com, the blundering president's drug use was made public when a former aide, the aptly named Douglas Wead, released tapes detailing Bush's drug history. Bush is quoted as saying, "I wouldn't answer the marijuana question. You know why? 'Cause I don't want some little kid doing what I tried. You gotta understand, I want to be president, I want to lead. Do you want your little kid to say 'Hey daddy, President Bush tried marijuana, I think I will?'" You probably do want that.

359. Change Is Coming

As you know, President Barack Obama is determined to avoid doing anything that President George W. Bush did. Obama took a page from Bill Clinton's book. Clinton admitted to having tried pot but said he "didn't inhale." Obama took things a step further and, according to the *New York Times*, said, "I did [inhale]. It's not something I'm proud of. It was a mistake as a young man. But I never understood [Clinton's] line. The point was to inhale." Obama's admission doesn't seem to have hurt him either. More young people voted in the 2008 election than ever before and, according to the Bureau of Justice, over 31 percent of college students have tried marijuana.

360. Trust the Court

You may know of Clarence Thomas as the second African American in history to ever sit on the Supreme Court, but his dream was in jeopardy when he admitted to smoking marijuana. According to the *Washington Post*, Thomas "took several puffs on a marijuana cigarette in college and perhaps once in law school. He believes it was a mistake and it was never repeated." He's held the post since 1991 and voiced his support for medicinal marijuana in 2005 when he wrote a dissent stating that it should be legalized and decriminalized in the state of California.

CHAPTER FIFTEEN

don't smoke those pages

Famous Baked Writers

"The biggest killer on the planet is stress and I still think the best medicine is and always has been cannabis."

—Stephen King, author

361. Jack Kerouac: On the Reefer Road

Let's be honest: if you're thinking about drug-using writers, Jack Kerouac will always be at the top of the list. Kerouac was a poet, painter, and writer, whose work has only gained in popularity since his death in 1969. Since then, his drug-soaked novel *On the Road* has become a bible for free spirits everywhere. Kerouac often wrote under the influence of marijuana and coined the term *beat generation*, which is characterized by the ideas of sexual revolution, respect for native cultures and nature, opposition of war, and the decriminalization of marijuana and other drugs. Kerouac's vision inspired his close friends Allen Ginsberg and William S. Burroughs, who also became well-known beat writers.

362. Allen Ginsberg: Pothead Waxing Poetic

Poet Allen Ginsberg was Kerouac's roommate at Columbia University and Kerouac inspired Ginsberg to seriously pursue poetry. Ginsberg's poem *Howl*, which was banned initially for its explicit descriptions and language, is viewed by many as a biography of the beat generation. Ginsberg was actually under the influence of marijuana and alcohol during his first reading of *Howl* at Reed College, which was documented by Kerouac in his novel *The Dharma Bums*. Ginsberg was also an avid supporter of drug legalization and worked closely with Timothy Leary to legalize LSD. Ginsberg was later deported from Cuba in 1965 for protesting Cuba's anti-marijuana laws and antihomosexual legislation.

363. Dr. Hunter S. Thompson: Gonzo, But Not Forgotten

Journalist, novelist, sometimes politician, and drug connoisseur Hunter S. Thompson is perhaps best known for his creation of the subjective "Gonzo journalism" and his well-known novel *Fear and Loathing in Las Vegas*. According to *High Times* magazine, Thompson said, "I have always loved marijuana. It has been a source of joy and comfort to me for many years. And I still think of it as a basic staple of life, along with beer and ice and grapefruits—and millions of Americans agree with me." Thompson tragically died of a self-inflicted gunshot wound in 2005. His remains were shot out of a cannon that was shaped like a peyote flower.

364. William Butler Yeats: Getting High with Dumas

You might not expect nineteenth-century Irish poet and politician William Butler Yeats to be on this list. Surprise! Just take a look at the topics of some of Yeats's best works and everything will begin to fall into place. Much of Yeats's poetry focuses on the world of spirits, fairies, and the creatures of Irish mythological lore.

He is credited as saying, "The mystical life is the centre of all that I do and all that I think and all that I write." Yeats became a member of the Hashish Club, which also boasts other famous members such as poet Arthur Symons and *The Three Musketeers* author Alexandre Dumas.

365. Mark Twain: Did Huck's Inventor Have a Thing for Hash?

There is some debate about whether Mark Twain (aka Samuel Clemens) ever actually partook in hashish. Why wouldn't Twain have given it a go? In fact, the *San Francisco Dramatic Chronicle* published an article in 1865 claiming that Twain was spotted high on hash. The article said, "It appears that a 'Hasheesh' mania has broken out among our Bohemians. Yesterday, Mark Twain and the 'Mouse-Trap' man [Tremenheere Lanyon Johns] were seen walking up Clay Street under the influence of the drug, followed by a 'star,' who was evidently laboring under a misapprehension as to what was the matter with them." You have to admit that sounds pretty conclusive.

366. Carl Sagan: Toke Up, See Space

Anyone who is into space this much has to be getting high on a regular basis. The astronomer and author of *Contact* is world-famous for his popular science books and the television series *Cosmos*. If you can imagine it, Carl Sagan's voice in the show was like a poor man's William Shatner. Although he never admitted it publicly, Sagan smoked pot regularly. He even wrote an essay about smoking cannabis in 1971 under a pseudonym. In this essay, Sagan states that pot enhanced his experiences and often influenced his writing.

367. Stephen King: Monster Dope Could Grow in Maine

Along with being the king of horror, Stephen King is also an avid supporter of drug law reform and has admitted to smoking pot in the past. Have you ever read his books stoned? It's definitely a scarier experience. He was quoted as saying, "I think that marijuana should not only be legal, I think it should be a cottage industry. It would be wonderful for the state of Maine. There's some pretty good homegrown dope. I'm sure it would be even better if you could grow it with fertilizers and have greenhouses." Maybe King's next novel will feature a smoke monster that haunts the DEA.

368. Louisa May Alcott: Forget Bongs, She'll Have a Bonbon

Daughter of transcendental revolutionaries and author of the beloved classic *Little Women*, Louisa May Alcott wrote about chocolates laced with hash in her story "Perilous Play." In it, a group of friends are offered hash by the local doctor, who says, "Eat six of these despised bonbons, and you will be amused in a new, delicious, and wonderful manner." You probably haven't had that sort of experience with bonbons without *something* being in them. Although Alcott never wrote about her personal experiences with pot, she might still have experimented in her time.

369. J. R. R. Tolkien: Lord of the Pipe

How else would someone come up with Middle Earth, Mordor, and Orcs if they weren't smoking some fine sheeba. J. R. R. Tolkien even made mention of smoking in the text of *The Lord of the Rings*. In the film and books, one of the hobbits' main hobbies was getting together with friends and smoking "pipe-weed." Also in one scene, the wizard Saruman criticizes Gandalf for smoking too much. He says, "Your love of the halflings' leaf has clearly slowed your mind." These scenes almost seem like Tolkien is describing you and your friends (except for the whole ring journey and being hobbits). Tolkien himself loved a good packed pipe. Now, whether it was filled with straight tobacco or wacky tobaccy, we'll never know.

370. William Shakespeare: Smoking His Stories

It hasn't been proven that William Shakespeare smoked weed, but researchers found fragments of pipes dating back to the seventeenth century near Shakespeare's garden that contain traces of cocaine and hallucinogenic drugs. It is also known that the cannabis plant was found in Elizabethan England, where it was used as fabric and paper. Now perhaps, Shakespeare was rolling up the sonnets and smoking them to get rid of writer's block. Also, some of his plays are pretty trippy—if you've read *Titus Andronicus*, you know the title character makes pies out of humans.

Literature You'll Never Be Too High to Read

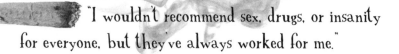

"I wouldn't recommend sex, drugs, or insanity for everyone, but they've always worked for me."

—Hunter S. Thompson, author

371. *It's Just a Plant*, by Ricardo Cortés (2005)

It's important to instill quality values in your children early on. Reading has always been both an educational and entertaining exercise and a bonding experience for children and their parents. So next time you're in the children's section of your favorite book store, pick up *It's Just a Plant* by Ricardo Cortés. This book claims to be nothing other than what it is—an illustrated children's book about marijuana. The story follows a young girl as she learns about the plant from a host of different characters, including her parents, a local farmer, a doctor, and a police officer. You'll be a good parent for informing your child about the world—just be careful what he or she writes about in next week's book report for school.

372. *Prozac Nation*, by Elizabeth Wurtzel (1994)

Before it was a box-office failure starring Christina Ricci, *Prozac Nation* was a best-selling novel by Elizabeth Wurtzel. Basically, the novel is a memoir following the author from childhood to adulthood while she battles severe depression and finds various means of relief. Naturally, the narrator tries just about every antidepressant under the sun, and of course spends a lot of time with a joint in her mouth. Really, who can be sad when they are stoned? With few exceptions, when you're high there aren't many problems that cannot be fixed by watching *The Big Lebowski*, right?

373. The Hitchhiker's Guide to the Galaxy, by Douglas Adams (1979)

The Hitchhiker's Guide to the Galaxy, the first book in the trilogy series of five books, is as out of this world as you can hope to be when you're high. Think about it: Arthur Dent is rescued by his alien friend Ford Prefect before Earth is destroyed because it is in the way of the new hyperspatial express route. Also, superintelligent alien mice created a supercomputer, "Deep Thought," that calculated the Question of Life, the Universe, and Everything to be "42," then created another computer called "Earth" to provide the question. Although there is no evidence that Douglas Adams actually smoked weed, he did call himself a "radical atheist," so he definitely would relate to stoner outcasts.

374. Fear and Loathing in Las Vegas, by Hunter S. Thompson (1972)

Hunter Stockton Thompson was perhaps the last great unabashed drug user in American media and is a weed role model for you and your friends. *Fear and Loathing in Las Vegas* follows a somewhat true story of Thompson's pseudonym Raoul Duke and his attorney on a drug-fueled search for the "American dream" in Las Vegas in the 1970s. Weed makes many appearances in the book, often used to calm the character's nerves after a dangerous, or "savage," incident. A few years before he died, Thompson was still smoking weed. In a 2003 interview with *High Times*, when asked if he still smoked weed, Thompson said, "Of course I do. Why would I quit? Smoking prevents Alzheimer's. That's why I'm still smoking."

375. Electric Kool-Aid Acid Test, by Tom Wolfe (1968)

Everyone knows that the '60s were an experimental time. Hippies from the East Coast to West Coast followed the out-there example set by Ken Kesey and his

Merry Pranksters. If you don't believe their antics from reading Kesey's own books (how much can he remember anyway?), take it from Tom Wolfe, who claims to have carried a notebook in hand while saying "no thank you" when LSD came around. His research is compiled in *The Electric Kool-Aid Acid Test* and—like it's a surprise—pot is mentioned numerous times along with any other drug that was popular during this mood-altering era.

376. Sometimes a Great Notion, by Ken Kesey (1964)

Ken Kesey has gone down in history as a wizard of weed. The man lived on a farm in Oregon with hundreds of followers. Whether or not his followers were physically and spiritually present, Kesey realized these people had an inherent interest in his alternative lifestyle. Whether you trust his authorial voice or not, Kesey's books like *Sometimes a Great Notion* should be required reading for serious stoners. Do yourself a favor: smoke up and escape to his out-of-this-universe world within the pages of his life.

377. On the Road, by Jack Kerouac (1957)

Jack Kerouac, the author responsible for pretty much reinventing literature in the 1940s with what later came to be called "beat" writing (i.e., beatnik), was an avid proponent of marijuana use. You might have had to read *On the Road* in high school. Basically a stream of consciousness story about Kerouac and his merry friends traveling across the country and their nights spent talking, philosophizing, drinking, and naturally, smoking copious amounts of weed.

378. *Howl*, by Allen Ginsberg (1956)

Allen Ginsberg's poem *Howl* has taken on mythical proportions in American literature. It sparked one of the nations first, and most important, obscenity trials because of it's language and portrayal of drug use. The lengthy, free-form poem is basically the poet's ode to his generation and country, which he felt was "destroyed by madness." He mentions weed many times throughout the poem, and tells of friends who were busted for simply having "a belt of marijuana" in New York. Does that ring true in your own life?

379. *Junky*, by William S. Burroughs (1953)

Pretty much all of William S. Burrough's novels consist of rampant drug use, but only *Junky* completely centers around it. Although for the most part it is a memoir chronicling Burrough's decades-long battle with heroin addiction, the book also contains a ton of matter-of-fact marijuana use. In fact, when no one in the book is talking about withdrawal symptoms, the characters are most likely having sex, drinking, or smoking lots and lots of weed. In a nutshell, the book provides you with the best reasons why you *should not* do heroin and the best reasons why you *should* smoke weed.

380. *The Sonnets*, by William Shakespeare (1609)

Back in 2001, scientists in South Africa set out to prove that Shakespeare himself used pot for inspiration. In pursuit of education, these stoner-intrigued scientists traveled to the garden of Shakespeare's original home in Stratford-upon-Avon.

Once there, the group dug up actual pipes, complete with traces of cannabis in them, and as a result their findings spread like wildfire through the press. Later a study published in the *South African Journal of Science* revealed that the excavation took place after a close rereading of Sonnet 76, which features a "noted weed." So if you want to believe it, Shakespeare was not only a wordsmith but also a pot smoker.

CHAPTER SIXTEEN

AROUND THE WORLD IN 80 TOKES

Travel Guide to a Cannabis Trip

"I was in Italy and then I took a balloon up my ass to Spain."

—Marijuana smuggler #2, played by John Ennis, on *Mr. Show with Bob and David*

381. Burning Man

Burning Man is the modern gold standard for any celebration of counterculture. The art event has been held in the middle of Nevada's Black Rock Desert every year since 1986. For eight days before Labor Day, tens of thousands of celebrants pour into the desert to inhabit a makeshift town. On Saturday night, a large wooden effigy of a man goes up in flames, giving the event its name. While it's not a marijuana event per se, it is a celebration of alternative lifestyles, which includes weed. There's no way you can prepare for the wildness that is Burning Man, but if you want to go, just be aware that there's no such thing as a spectator there.

382. Hash Bash

Held at high noon (rhymes *and* puns, how can you go wrong?) on the first Saturday of every April, Ann Arbor's Hash Bash is a laid-back celebration of marijuana consumption. The event takes place in the University of Michigan's Diag, where several thousand students and visitors light up together. Possession of marijuana on university property is technically illegal, but arrests are relatively rare and are usually for offenses such as disorderly conduct. Hash Bash began as a peaceful smoke-in event in 1972 to honor a state Supreme Court ruling that made possession of marijuana a misdemeanor instead of a felony. If you have a hobby of collecting marijuana paraphernalia, the accompanying Monroe Street Fair that features live shows and booths will give you your fix.

383. Seattle Hempfest

Since 1991, the Seattle Hempfest has done its best to educate the public about the benefits of marijuana, battle the stigma of marijuana use, and advocate for reform of marijuana laws. It basically provides you with ammunition to prove DARE wrong. People smoke up regularly at the "protestival," but the Seattle police department were focused on other priorities even before a successful 2003 ballot initiative to de-prioritize prosecution of marijuana possession. Every August, you can rub shoulders with hundreds of thousands of fellow cannabis enthusiasts and listen to high-profile speakers such as actor Woody Harrelson and travel guru Rick Steves, who have helped raise the profile of the event. The two-day festival takes place in Myrtle Edwards Park.

384. Global Marijuana March

The Global Marijuana March is a cooperative, international effort to focus attention on legalizing marijuana. In 2009, 267 cities participated. It began in 1999 and has included a total of more than 500 cities in more than 50 countries. Also known as the Million Marijuana March, the event is held the first Saturday in May every year. Organizers in individual cities rely on social networking and old-fashioned word of mouth to publicize the event, and participants actively help with funding, publicity, cleanup, and entertainment. Even if the March is unsuccessful, you'll still be able to philosophize the failure of the event with your fellow still-stoned participants.

385. 4/20 Celebrations

Every year on April 20, marijuana enthusiasts gather to celebrate and share their love of marijuana. Celebrations are not coordinated, but organizers in cities all over the world take it upon themselves to plan parties and other events. Popular events include the annual screening of *The Big Lebowski* at the Red Vic Theater in San Francisco at 4:20 P.M. and organized mayhem at the Vancouver Art Gallery. In 2008, about 10,000 people lit up on the University of Colorado's North Quadrangle for a 4/20 event. Police did not cite any of them for their technically illegal actions, so if you're a senior in high school and have started searching for colleges, you should seriously consider the University of Colorado.

386. Hanfparade

Billed as the largest marijuana festival in Europe, Hanfparade follows on the heels of Berlin's famed Love Parade every summer. Hundreds of thousands of marijuana enthusiasts take to the streets of Berlin every August to call for the legalization of cannabis. Hanfparade began in 1997 when 10,000 people joined together to march on the Brandenburg Gate and demand legalization. Although police keep a careful eye on the event, you'll be able to party with the revelers and might even be hidden by all of the smoke in the air anyway. Also, Hanfparade produces positive vibes with colorful floats, friendly participants, and pro-marijuana speeches.

387. Boston Freedom Rally

If you're in New England, the Boston Freedom Rally is the East Coast's version of the Seattle Hempfest. It has been held at high noon on the third Saturday of September every year since 1989. The historic Boston Common has hosted the event since 1995, and MassCann/NORML organizes it. More than 100,000 people show up to hear live performances and speeches. Vendors and activists raise public awareness of the benefits of marijuana and draw attention to the need for legislation reform. The 2009 rally celebrated twenty years of rallying for cannabis as well as a new Massachusetts statute decriminalizing the possession of less than an ounce of marijuana; it's about time for this rebellious state—after all, Massachusetts was the only state that didn't vote for Richard Nixon in the 1972 election.

388. Great Midwest Marijuana Harvest Festival

Going strong for almost four decades, the Great Midwest Marijuana Harvest Festival takes over the streets of Madison, Wisconsin, for three days every October. Crowds gather to listen to speeches, march from Liberty Mall to the Capitol, and rally for the legalization of cannabis. Since it falls about a month before election day, you'll probably hear a lot about the importance of voting, especially in election years. Smoking at the event is technically illegal; however, since the timing coincides with college football season, Madison's police force is often split between the University of Wisconsin's campus and the festival, so you might have some leeway. Also, thankfully, you don't have to wear a cheesehead to this festival.

389. Toronto Freedom Festival

The Toronto Freedom Festival is technically a celebration of freedom in general, but a large part of it focuses on the freedom to smoke marijuana. Celebrating just its third anniversary in 2009, it drew 30,000 revelers to Queens Park on a rainy Saturday in May. It features live music, speeches, and cannabis education at the *High Times* magazine Vendors Village. A separate CALM-Medical Marijuana Pavillion provides information on the benefits of using marijuana for medicinal purposes. Also, although Canadians are born with ice skates on their feet, you will not have to skate while high at any point during the festival.

390. Cannabis Revival

Cannabis Revival, held in Joplin, Missouri, is a celebration of marijuana that features live music, art, and speeches. Organized by NORML's Joplin chapter, the event has been held every year in September since 1997. If you've somehow attended all of the events mentioned in this chapter, you probably know all about legalizing marijuana and educating the public about the benefits of medicinal marijuana by now. However, the 2005 event also showcased a car that was powered by hemp biodiesel, and that rocks.

The Greatest Smoking Places

"It's illegal to carry it, but that doesn't really matter 'cause get a load of this, all right—if you get stopped by the cops in Amsterdam, it's illegal for them to search you. I mean, that's a right the cops in Amsterdam don't have."

—Vincent Vega, played by John Travolta, in *Pulp Fiction*

391. Amsterdam, of Course

Long considered the world's cannabis capital, Amsterdam should be on every serious toker's must-see list. You can legally purchase marijuana at one of the city's numerous coffeeshops (uppers and downers for your delight!). According to Dutch law, they're allowed to sell five grams of weed to patrons over the age of eighteen. They're not permitted to advertise, so check out the Amsterdam Coffeeshop Directory at *www.coffeeshop.freeuk.com* for maps, reviews, and forums. Many of the shops are nestled together in the midst of the city's famous red light district, which makes it easy for you to catch a show and buy some weed in one fell swoop. Also, the Hash, Marijuana, and Hemp Museum is the perfect museum to visit if you've just smoked a bowl.

392. Mexico, Amigo

Mexican drug cartels make about $8.5 billion a year from trafficking marijuana, so why not go directly to the source? Marijuana is cheap and easy to find in many of Mexico's spring break meccas, including Acapulco, Tijuana, and Cabo. However, for all of these benefits, you'll find some hazards that will kill your buzz. You might be tempted to pass a joint around on the beach, but the police patrol public areas. On the upside, if you haven't spent all of your money on tequila and weed, you probably will be able to bribe the police. Also, the quality of Mexican drugs and dealers is really sketchy (even when you're high), so choose wisely.

393. Brazil—Rio, Baby!

Beautiful beaches. Legendary party places. Carnaval. Brazil is a natural vacation destination for the marijuana enthusiast. Although you have to be careful to avoid law enforcement personnel (you don't want to end up in prison period, but especially if it's a Brazilian prison) and bud isn't as easy to score here as it is in other places, Brazil's party atmosphere makes it worth the trip. Carnaval, the unparalleled celebration that takes place for four days every year before Lent, is known around the world for its extreme debauchery, a perfect trip for a pothead. Urban Rio has it all—beaches, culture, and parties—but don't underestimate other places on Brazil's long coastline like Florianopolis in the south and Bahia in the north.

394. Costa Rica, Tourist Trap?

Costa Rica's mountainous north and south regions are perfect for growing pot— and that's what many people do. Until fairly recently, it wasn't illegal to grow small amounts of marijuana, and weed is still widely available in the country. Unfortunately, new legislation takes a much harder line, but the good news is that weed comrades who you're likely to run into are very tolerant of marijuana use. However, you should be aware that local dealers sometimes cooperate with the police to set up stings for tourists. Also, the gorgeous rainforests and world-class beaches are the perfect visiting spots if your hotel room is getting too smoky.

395. Czech Republic, Go to Prague for Pot

Prague in particular is lenient when it comes to weed. You'll relate to the unsuccessful attempts of the very vocal segment of the Czech population that is pushing for the legalization of marijuana. Street dealers usually aren't reputable (are they really ever?), but there are cafés and bars where you'll be able to make some contacts. Taxi drivers are also good sources of information—even the mayor of Prague, Pavel Bém, discovered this firsthand when he rode his city's taxis in disguise to check on their service.

396. Israel, Value Weed

The Holy Land may not seem like a natural place to smoke up, but the weed here is relatively inexpensive and good quality. While it is illegal, the police usually have bigger problems to worry about. Your best bets for scoring weed are in the resort cities near the beaches and clubs. Tel Aviv is also a good place. There is a push to legalize marijuana, and the 2009 elections featured the rather bizarre Holocaust Survivors' and Grown-Up Green Leaf Party, whose platform was based on "personal freedom, quality of life, and decriminalization and legalization of all applications of the cannabis plant." The group did not win any seats in the Knesset.

397. California, Mecca of Medicinal Marijuana

Marijuana is estimated to be a multibillion-dollar industry in the state of California. Much of it comes from the Emerald Triangle in Northern California and is legal under state law. In 1996, California became the first state to legalize medical marijuana, and in February 2009, San Francisco assemblyman Tom Ammiano introduced a bill in the state legislature that would legalize all marijuana. Also, Arnold Schwarzenegger, the governor of California, has been nicknamed "the Governator." Next time you're high (well, now), say this word over and over. Now, say it with Arnold's Austrian accent. Yeah, that's right.

398. Hawaii–Hang Ten, Get High

The Aloha State and its *lei*d-back attitude are perfect for living the high life. If you're lucky enough to make friends on one of the islands, you might be lucky enough to score an invite to a bonfire on the beach. Your best bet is probably someone who acts like Paul Rudd's surfing instructor in *Forgetting Sarah Marshall*. You do need to keep an eye out for the police, who patrol the beaches and other public areas regularly. It's illegal to sell marijuana under any circumstances, but people with medical certificates are allowed to cultivate marijuana in their own homes.

399. Canadian Rockies, Land of Cannabis

Ever wondered what a bona fide Rocky Mountain high feels like? It's easy enough to find out. Breathtaking ski runs, awe-inspiring scenery, and high-quality cannabis make this a great place to visit. There's a reason all the professional snowboarders you watch on Versus look perpetually stoned. However, a run-in with a real live Canadian Mountie might seem like a good idea when you're high, but it really is not (especially when you keep asking him if you can wear his hat). However, enforcement of marijuana laws is relatively relaxed, so you probably won't have to worry about running into Mounties anyway.

400. England—Turf Tavern Then on to Kebabs!

Stuffy Britannia is known more for tea leaves than marijuana, but its population of university students knows how to indulge. Tucked away on a narrow, winding street, Oxford's ancient Turf Tavern is famous for being the place where future president Bill Clinton neglected to inhale back when he was a Rhodes scholar. The Turf's low ceilings, haphazard layout, and excellent selection of draft beers make it somewhat difficult to navigate if you're high. You can tumble back out to the main streets to satisfy your munchies at one of Oxford's ubiquitous kebab stands, which dish out everything from poutine to fries to, naturally, kebabs.

CHAPTER SEVENTEEN

*oh, the PLACES you'll go . . .
or Avoid*

Hash Hangouts

"I used to smoke marijuana. But I'll tell you something: I would only smoke it in the late evening. Oh, occasionally the early evening, but usually the late evening—or the mid-evening. Just the early evening, mid-evening and late evening. Occasionally, early afternoon, early mid-afternoon, or perhaps the late-mid-afternoon. Oh, sometimes the early-mid-late-early morning . . . but never at dusk."

—Steve Martin, actor and comedian

401. Your Parents' Basement Is More Than a Storage Unit

It smells of mothballs, laundry detergent, and damp concrete. The hockey uniform you wore the last year of high school is dangling from a clothes hanger in the corner. And the television's the old small-screen one with the remote that only works when you hold it up and to the left of the TV. But the great thing is, you've got privacy. Now's the time to light up, turn on the fan to blow the smoke out the window, and watch reruns of *The Fresh Prince of Bel-Air* (for extra fun while high, exclaim, "Will Smith," every time he acts like a smartass). And if your father does start to wander downstairs, be sure to have a handy place to stash your joint (see Chapter 7).

402. The Video Arcade Isn't Just for Geeks

You have to be careful here, because there are a lot of people around, and management isn't thrilled by the sight of someone sparking up right next to the Super Mario Brothers console. But a couple of quiet minutes in the john with a joint and you're ready to face the flashing lights, the buzzers, the bells, the sounds of gunfire, and racing autos. However, the fighting games, like Mortal Kombat, might freak you out, so try and stick with the nonbloody games.

403. A Ferris Wheel Will Get You High, Then Low, Then High . . .

The cool thing about this is that you've got some privacy. Nobody's going to try to bust you when you're two hundred feet in the air. And what could be cooler than getting stoned when the whole town and the lights from the carnival are spread out below you? Of course, it's probably going to be more fun going up than coming down, when you may hallucinate that you're falling, but as long as you can keep from screaming too loudly and possibly freaking out, you should be good.

404. At the Aquarium, You'll Be Jealous of Every Animal's Life

The aquarium is so peaceful and quiet that it's the perfect place to go when you're high. You'll have your pick of which specimens, from Atlantic Harbor seals to African penguins, to see stoned. You can stare into the tanks for hours just thinking about how you would like to seamlessly swim like a North Atlantic right whale or chillax like a green sea turtle. Also, most of the animals, like sea dragons and cownose rays, seem like they're naturally stoned anyway. "Oh," you'll also think to yourself, "if I owned a moon jelly, my life would be complete."

405. The Planetarium: The Lights and the Sound, Man!

This is truly the greatest stoner experience that you will have ever. Ever. Whether it's LaserFloyd or anything space-themed, you're sure to feel, ahem, out of this world. The lights across the dome and the trippy music will make you not notice that you're drooling at the awesomeness. However, make sure you don't make the mistake the freaks in *Freaks and Geeks* (yes, Judd Apatow again) made and accidentally get a cowboy light show with "The Devil Went Down to Georgia" instead of Pink Floyd. That's just not right.

406. Wait, Do People Actually Watch Golf Tournaments Sober?

Let's face it: Watching paint dry is more exciting. Some guy hits a tiny white ball, it goes about two hundred feet, and then he walks over to it and hits it again. Now just imagine how much more interesting all this will get if you're high as a kite. Also, there are plenty of places to spark up: the clubhouse, the public bathrooms, behind the sand trap on the fourteenth hold. However, you might still be bored out of your mind, unless you're actually watching *Caddyshack.*

407. Disneyland: Making a Difference for the First Time Since You Were Eight

What could be more surreal than the Happiest Place on Earth? A sunlit tract jammed with crowds clad in Bermuda shorts, where you might turn a corner and run head-on into Goofy or Minnie or even Mickey himself. A place where on Mr. Toad's Wild Ride, you go hurtling through doors that open at the last minute and see huge mutant badgers and rats coming around corners at you. Disneyland without drugs is just an incredible simulation of a Magical Kingdom. But with a couple of joints in your pocket to be safely smoked in a bathroom stall or discretely around the corner from Splash Mountain, it will really become the Magical Kingdom.

408. Nepal, Where You Can Get Your High and Meditation On

Yes, it is a little remote. But imagine sitting cross-legged on a mountain, puffing on a joint, and watching the sunrise over the Himalayas. Smoking and cultivation was legal in Nepal until the 1970s, and even now it's tolerated without much harassment. The locals smoke weed to celebrate Lord Shiva's birthday, and holy men in the temples use hash for an extra dose of wisdom. You can pick up some good hash in Kathmandu, then sit outside, light up, and let your mind expand with the mountains. And remember: you're only doing what thousands of hippies did before you in the 1960s.

409. Jamaica: Is It Legal *Not* to Smoke Weed There?

Well, the only problem with going to Jamaica to get high is that you might get murdered. This city has the highest rate for violent deaths in the Caribbean. But if you can get over that, it's the most authentic Rastafarian experience you can get. Smoking is tolerated, and the police are easily bribable. And weed is *everywhere*. Also, to truly satisfy your munchies while there, you should watch the Jamaican episode of *Anthony Bourdain: No Reservations* and take all of Bourdain's recommendations to heart.

410. Paris: You Will Fully Appreciate Your Love for Your Weed

It's the City of Light. And it's *French*! Just being in the city is a high in itself. As long as you're discrete, you can inhale by the side of the Seine, puff while strolling through the Hall of Mirrors in Versailles (and where could you ask for a more trippy experience than the hall of mirrors?), or stand at the top of the Eiffel Tower, take a hit off your joint, and stare down at Paris for, oh, two or three hours maybe.

No Potheads Allowed

Kumar Patel (Kal Penn): Hang on a second, nurse. What we should probably use is marijuana. That'll sufficiently sedate the patient for surgery.
Male Nurse (Ryan Reynolds): Marijuana? But why?
Kumar: We don't have time for questions. We need marijuana now, as much of it as possible! Like a big bag of it.

—*Harold and Kumar Go to White Castle*

411. High Times Under the Big Top

Why's that clown laughing at me? That guy's going to fall! I can't swallow this cotton candy! Sure, a circus *seems* like a cool place to go when you're baked out of your mind, but think of the three-ring paranoia that's going to set in once you take your seat in the stands. With way too much happening, an insane amount of noise, and a whole lot of dads giving you the evil eye, blazing before the Ringling Bros. is sure to be anything but fun. Stay home, hit the bubbler, and watch *Dumbo*—much safer.

412. Not in *His* House

It's understandable: getting high brings you to a higher plane of spirituality and you want to reach out to the big guy upstairs by going to church. However, the power of pot-induced prayer is better suited for your home rather than the house of God. Beyond the fact that you're almost certain to pass out during the service, the possibility of openly weeping, giggling during the homily, or choking on the communion wafer are all reasons not to follow up on your friend's suggestion of "Dude, we should go to Mass." Jesus, Mary, and Joseph will all be much happier if you spend your Sunday stoned on your couch.

413. Happy Birthday to . . . Whom?

The last thing your grandma (and mom and uncle and cousin and . . .) wants to see the day she turns ninety is your bleary red eyes staring off into space as you wish her a Merry Christmas. Showing up high to your grandma's birthday party is one of the worst things you can do. Besides being pegged as the family pothead—taking the title away from free-spirited Auntie Annie—think how awful and awkward "normal" conversation is at family get-togethers. Now think how bad it would be baked. Yeah. Even if Granny tokes up to beat her glaucoma, there's a time and place to share your love of dank headies.

414. Stay Away from the All-You-Can-Eat Buffet

I know what you're thinking: *Are you crazy? An all-you-can-eat buffet is a great idea!* It is—when you're stoned. Satisfying your munchies after a session is always a ton of fun. However, this is just some forward-thinking for you, and the way you'll feel after a faded feast at an all-you-can-eat buffet will be enough for you to swear off the sticky forever (or at least a month). When does a plate piled high with crab Rangoon mixed with buffalo chicken on top of pasta Alfredo with a side of cornbread sound like a delicious decision? When you're high. What's it sound like when you're not high? A one-way ticket on the porcelain express.

415. Office Spaced

Work sure does suck. But unless you work at Empire Records or as Lil Wayne's personal assistant, do not go to work high. It won't make work suck less. It won't make the day go by faster. It won't make your coworkers any more tolerable. Okay, so maybe the last one was a lie . . . but being high at work is not something you want to endure. You know how paranoid you get when you think the cashier at Taco Bell suspects you're high? Multiply that by a million and that's how paranoid you'll be when you start thinking your boss knows you're high.

416. Spinning Out of Control

Similar to the all-you-can-eat buffet, going to a record store *sounds* like a great idea. And if you have a ton of cash, it is. However, your smoke session has left you with little self-control, and flipping through a bunch of vinyl isn't the most financially sound adventure. Like the buffet, you'll enjoy indulging in excess while high but when you wake from your stone-coma, you'll realize the error of your ways. You blew all your money on rare reissues and hard-to-find originals, and now you don't even have enough cash for a dime bag.

417. Fried on Facebook

This entry takes the Reader Beware to the digital landscape. Just as dangerous as writing e-mails while intoxicated, clicking over to the Book while baked is dangerous. Not only will you spend hour upon hour mindlessly navigating through profile page and wall and group listings, but you'll also realize the next day that your friend list has grown considerably (or at least your number of friend requests has). The kid who played left field on your little league team? Friended. That girl from your Intro to Chem class that you never spoke a word to? Friended. Your boss's husband? Friended. And you? Embarrassed—hopefully.

418. The DMV? WTF?

Yeah, yeah, the DMV is an easy comic target and—like everything else—has been beaten like a dead horse by Dane Cook. But *really*, when you're stoned, the DMV is hell. You might think, *But I'm just going to be standing there for a few hours. . . . Where's the harm?* Do. Not. Do. It. The stress of waiting plus the "friendliness" of the clerks multiplied by the paperwork and hundred other people waiting will kill whatever mellow attitude you may assume while stoned and send you into the throws of a serious panic attack.

419. Not the Right Move

If you've never experienced seeing a serious movie in the theaters while high, you might want to try this one out. Except don't be the high one. Get one of your friends high and bring them to the latest tear-jerker. Then as the crucial moment approaches when the story's protagonist passes away from a terminal illness, or tells her child that she's passing away from a terminal illness, or watches her child pass away from a terminal illness, and your friend cracks up laughing, you will be able to feel the rage of every moviegoer in that theater. While the rage may not manifest into physical harm (if he's lucky), it's a serious karma-killer. Boo, man.

420. *Definitely* Not the Right Move

What's worse than ruining a serious movie with a bout of uncalled-for laughter? Ruining a hilarious movie with a bout of uncalled-for laughter. No one wants to hear some fried pothead laugh out loud between jokes just because he realized that the main character's wearing shorts, and that's funny for whatever reason. There's a time and place for busting out laughing while high at a comedy. It's called three months later on your couch. Save yourself a world of hurt; these aren't the same pansies who were on the verge of tears over a terminal illness—they'll kick your ass.

SOURCES

www.420magazine.com

www.abcnews.com

www.amsterdam.info

The Associated Press

www.boston.com

www.bostonfreedomrally.com

Boston Globe

Boston Herald

Boulder Daily Camera

www.cannabis.com

www.cannabisnews.com

www.cinema-astoria.com

www.comedycentral.com

www.crrh.org

CNBC.com

CNN.com

www.drugpolicy.org

www.drugwarfacts.org

www.ecofibre.com.au

www.erowid.org

www.espn.go.com

E-stoned.com

Exposay.com

www.foxnews.com

www.Friendsofcannabis.com

www.Gone-hollywood.com

GQ Magazine

www.hanfparade.de

www.hempcar.org

Herer, Jack. *The Emperor Wears No Clothes: The Authoritative Historical Record of Cannabis and the Conspiracy Against Marijuana.* Oakland: Quirk American Archives, 2000.

www.Hightimes.com

www.Huffingtonpost.com

www.humboldtmirror.wordpress.com

www.independent.co.uk

Isralowitz, Richard. *Drug Use, Policy, and Management*. Santa Barbara, CA: Greenwood, 2002.

www.makingbongs.com

www.marijuana.com

Mathre, Mary Lynn. *Cannabis in Medical Practice: A Legal, Historical and Pharmacological Overview of the Therapeutic Use of Marijuana*. Jefferson, NC: McFarland, 1997.

www.metro.us/us/home

www.msnbc.msn.com

www.naihc.org

news.bbc.co.uk

New York Daily News

www.november.org

People magazine

www.postchronicle.com

www.premiere.com

www.rawstory.com

www.rense.com

Rubin, Vera. *Cannabis and Culture*. Berlin: Mouton De Gruyter, 1975.

www.seattletimes.com

www.Slate.com

San Francisco Chronicle

www.SpliffMagazine.com

St. Clair, Jeffrey, and Alexander Cockburn. *Whiteout: The CIA, Drugs, and the Press*. New York: Verso, 1999.

TheStonersCookbook.com

http://stopthedrugwar.org

Swanson, Tim. *Entourage: A Lifestyle Is a Terrible Thing to Waste*. New York: Pocket Books, 2007.

www.torontofreedomfestival.com

www.upi.com

www.usatoday.com

Washington Post

www.wayodd.com

www.wbbm780.com

www.youtube.com

Contributors

Peter Archer
Laura Casasanto
Katie Corcoran Lytle
Matt Glazer
Scott Glazer
Elizabeth Kassab
Chelsea King
Jason Niemann
Andrea Norville
Meredith O'Hayre
Brendan O'Neill
Wendy Simard

Acknowledgments

Thanks to everybody at Adams Media for helping to make this book possible, with special thanks to Paula Munier, Casey Ebert, Matt LeBlanc, Beth Gissinger, Elisabeth Lariviere, and Heather M. Padgen.